Thank You
for your support!

THE STORY OF ONE MARINE
The World War I Letters and Photos of Pvt. Thomas L. Stewart
©2017 James P. Gregory, Jr.

Published by Hellgate Press
(An imprint of L&R Publishing, LLC)

Hellgate Press
PO Box 3531
Ashland, OR 97520
email: sales@hellgatepress.com

Editor: Harley B. Patrick
Interior design: Michael Campbell
Cover design: L. Redding

ISBN 978-1-55571-879-4

THE STORY OF ONE MARINE

*The World War I Letters and
Photos of Pvt. Thomas L. Stewart*

Edited by

JAMES P. GREGORY, JR.

In memory of
David Woodson Kirk

CONTENTS

*Of course it's not a picnic to charge thru a field
or wood swept with a machine gun and artillery
barrage, but it doesn't last long, and, after
all, is the greatest game of them all, and the
Americans are the best sportsmen.*

THOMAS L. STEWART

PREFACE

ON APRIL 6, 2017, the United States celebrates the 100th anniversary of joining the First World War. Once the United States joined the war, it was only 19 months until the surrender of Germany. Throughout those months, the US brought in more than four million soldiers to partake in the war, with half of those participating overseas. Out of that four million, more than nine thousand Marines served overseas.[1]

Thomas L. Stewart enlisted in the Marine Corps on June 27, 1917 at Paris Island, South Carolina. From the day he boarded the train to Paris Island to his last day in Europe, Tom sent home letters to his family. These letters shed light on what he did in training, the deployment overseas, battles against the Germans, his wounding, Military Police (MP) duty in France at the hospital, the armistice, his time at the American University in Beaune, travel across France, his travel back to his company, and Occupation Force duty on the Rhine. These letters describe his thoughts and actions as the war progressed around him. However, not all of these survive today. Luckily, Tom's sister, Vera, transcribed the letters during, or shortly after, the war. Then, in the early 2000's, Tom's daughter, Carolyn, transcribed Vera's copies into Microsoft Word, thus saving them and making them easily accessible for my research.

Tom also carried a Kodak camera with him during his training at Paris Island, South Carolina and at Quantico, Virginia, during his time as an MP, and during his time occupying Germany. These provide a unique view into his life as he saw it 100 years ago. The letters are transcribed from the original documents and

---

1   Mitchell Yockelson, "They Answered the Call: Military Service in the United States Army During World War I, 1917-1919," *Prologue* 30, no. 3 (Fall 1998), www.archives.org.

incorporated in their original form with misspellings, punctuation errors, and notations. Many primary and secondary sources are incorporated to create a more complete record of this Marine as he was a very humble man who did not speak of his service nor the great battles in which he fought. Being so humble, this book aims to tell his story and show how this one Marine played a role in some of the most decisive battles of the war.

I want to thank the entire Stewart and Kirk family for preserving these documents and Tom's history for the last 100 years and allowing me to access all of the records. I also want to thank Carolyn Stewart Kirk for her work in transcribing the letters and storing all the documents and photos for future generations. I would also like to thank David Kirk for his work in recording an interview with his grandfather, Tom, in the 1980's. It was a great fountain of information directly from the source. I also owe many thanks to Mr. Steven C. Girard, SSG, USA (Ret) for all the help in identifying the photographs taken by Tom, providing captions, and pointing me in the right direction for research whenever I got stuck; without him, I would not have been able to do justice to Tom's legacy. His knowledge and extreme willingness to help has been the greatest source of inspiration while writing. I also want to thank Mr. Kevin Seldon for his help. Also, I'd like to thank James Carl Nelson for the help in finding some research for the book. Finally, I'd like to thank Lenny Moore for help in identifying other soldiers in Tom's photos.

PEOPLE MENTIONED IN RELATION TO TOM STEWART

Bob: Margaret Stewart, *sister*

Bob Hood: From Hutchinson, Kansas, *a "flame" of Lois*

Deac: Vernon "Deke" Ward from Spearville, Kansas, *friend*

Doc: James Vivian "Viv" Stewart, *brother*

Dorto: Dorothy Stewart, *sister*

Elizabeth: Elizabeth Leidigh, *cousin*

Em: Emma Leidigh, *aunt*

Folks: Dora Leidigh Stewart and Van Stewart, *mom and dad*

Granny: Grandmother Leidigh, *grandma*

Harry: Harry Leidigh, *uncle*

Helen: Helen Stewart, *sister*

Junior: Harry Leidigh Jr., *cousin*

Katherine: Katherine Leidigh, *cousin*

Lois: Lois Stewart, *sister*

Po: Florence Leidigh (Merrick), *aunt*

Stanley: Stanley Williams from Spearville, Kansas, *friend*

Ted: Theodore Stewart, *brother*

Tom: Tom Westmacott from Spearville, Kansas, *friend*

Vee: Vera Stewart, *sister*

INTRODUCTION
PRE-WAR AND AMERICAN LEAD-UP

THOMAS LEIDIGH STEWART was born on March 6, 1895 in Spearville, Kansas, to Van and Dora Leidigh Stewart. He was the fourth child of eight, but the first son, to Dora and Van—older sisters Vera (1887), Helen (1889), and Lois (1893), younger brother James "Viv" (1899), younger sisters Dorothy (1902) and Margaret (1903), and youngest brother Ted (1905). He grew up in a small town with a population of around 600 people. His mother kept him from school until he was 7 years old because she needed help with his younger brother and sister. However, he managed to make the grades and graduate on time.

Tom was in the first graduating class of Spearville High School in 1913 as one of six seniors. After graduation, he went to work at the First National Bank in Spearville, which his family owned. Once he had saved enough money, he attended Colorado College from Fall 1913 to Spring 1915. While there, he became a member of the Phi Delta Theta fraternity. Around this time, he also joined the Masonic lodge under the Order of the Eastern Star. Once he returned to Spearville, Tom moved in with his Grandmother Leidigh. He then worked at the large general store in town for a while until accepting a job back at First National Bank as a bookkeeper.

The War

Austria's Arch Duke, Franz Ferdinand, was assassinated on June 28, 1914 in Sarajevo, Bosnia. This caused a wave of violence to race across Europe as blame was thrown from one country to another. The culmination of this blame was the Great War. Russia, Germany, France, Great Britain, the Austro Hungarians, and the Ottoman Empire waged massive all-out war on each other, ruining the picturesque landscapes of Europe and the Middle East. By 1917, the war had been raging for over 3 years. It pushed rapid industrialization as new machines of war were deployed in great numbers across three continents. Along with the machines, innovative methods of warfare were developed to combat the devastating firepower the machines could put out. Trenches became the means of transportation, message relay, and defense as they proved to be safe out of sight of the enemy scopes. Trench networks spread over 500 miles from the English Channel to the border of Switzerland. This created a stalemate as neither side could dislodge the opponent from their position.

The United States avoided being dragged into the quagmire of the European War. Instead, the US sold aid to France and Great Britain. However, as the aid increased, the Germans began using submarines, called U-boats, to track and attack the American shipments in the Atlantic Ocean. By 1917, these attacks had escalated to a point that the Americans could not ignore them any longer.

On top of the U-boat attacks, the United States faced another threat below their own border with Mexico. Pancho Villa, a Mexican revolutionary, raided the southern territory of the US around Columbus, New Mexico, killing eight soldiers and nine civilians. This caused U.S. President Woodrow Wilson to send the army under Brigadier General John Pershing into Mexico to pursue Villa.[2]

On March 1, 1917, President Wilson made the Zimmerman telegram public. This was a telegram from German Foreign Secretary Alfred Zimmerman to the German ambassador in Mexico. It proposed a military alliance between Germany and Mexico

---

2   Thomas Boghardt, "Chasing Ghosts in Mexico: The Columbus Raid of 1916 and the Politicization of U.S. Intelligence during World War I," *Army History* (Fall 2013): 7-10.

in the event that the United States declared war on Germany. It promised the return of Texas, New Mexico, and Arizona to Mexico at the end of the war.[3] Then, on March 18, President Wilson learned that German submarines had sunk three American ships in the English Channel as they headed back towards Texas.[4] On April 6, 1917 the United States Congress declared war upon Germany.

The nation now prepared to go to war. No one could envision how great the American war contribution would be but the nation began to collect supplies and manpower. American citizens started to see the war as a duty to not only country but to the security of the world. Thomas Stewart was another young American, 22 at the time, who saw war service as his duty. The following letter, documents, and memoir excerpts show how he and his family prepared for the upcoming conflict.

Excerpt from a letter to Van from Tom's aunt Minnie Stewart, May 2, 1917.

My Dear Van,

I made some good resolutions the first of the year about writing letters to the home folks, but guess I am getting behind. It hardly seems like the 2nd of May, for it is quite cold and we are still wearing winter wraps. Occasionally we have a few warm days, but they don't last. People haven't much garden made yet, but there will be more than usual made this year, as it looks like we would need all the eatables we could get in any way to feed our own people and the Allies, etc. I still, as we all did, hoped that we could keep out of the terrible War, but I guess for humanity's sake, as well as our own Country's, we

---

3   Byron Farwell, *Over There: The United States in the Great War, 1917-1918* (New York: W.W. Norton and Company, 1999), 33-34.

4   Frank Freidel, *Over There: The Story of America's First Great Overseas Crusade* (New York: McGraw-Hill, 1990), 4.

will have to enter into it for all we are worth. I think the German Rulers are out to conquer the world, if they can. I am wondering whether any of the Stewart boys will have to enlist. It seems dreadful to think of all War means, especially this War.

Minnie Stewart

Excerpt from Tom's Memoir

Young men knew they had a duty and mulled over what branch of the service was best for them. By May, Tom Westmacott, Deke Ward, and myself went to Wichita to join up for Officers training. They wanted only college graduates and Deke was the only one. We were told that we would be notified and we went back home but none was accepted.

Tom and his friends went on May 10, 1917 with letters of recommendation when they attempted to apply for Officers training. Even though they were not accepted, two of these surviving letters affirm Tom's character and his abilities.

Letter of Recommendation for Tom from P.T. Westmacott, May 10, 1917

To Whom It May Concern:

This is to certify that Thomas Leidigh Stewart was in our employ for two years, and I can say without question that he is steady and industrious. His morals and character are of the best and he commands the greatest respect of all with whom he comes in contact. It is with pleasure that I am able to give this un-reserved recommendation.

Yours truly,
The Edwards & Nichols Lbr. And Sup. Co.
P.T. Westmacott
Treasurer

Letter of Recommendation for Tom from Unknown Signature, May 7, 1917

Dear Sir,

I am writing to recommend Mr. T. L. Stewart of Spearville, Kansas.

Mr. Stewart was a student at Colorado College. He has unusual ability and strength of character and should make an efficient officer. He would command the respect of his men. I recommend him without reservation.

Sincerely yours,
Unknown Signature

Excerpt from Tom's Memoir

On June 5th all young men were to register for the draft so I went to Dodge City to register, it was a rainy day and I spent the afternoon in a hotel lobby waiting for the train home, after the few minutes registering.

As these letters and documents show, Tom was ready to do his part for the war. After signing up for the draft, less than a month passed before he and his friends, Stanley Williams and Deke Ward, traveled to Wichita, Kansas to enlist in the United States Marine Corps.

CHAPTER ONE
ENLISTMENT

AFTER FAILING TO QUALIFY for officer training, Tom and his friends decided that they would not just sit idly by and wait to be drafted. On June 20, 1917, Tom, Stanley Williams, and Deke Ward traveled to the Marine recruiting station in Wichita, Kansas. Tom was 22 years old at this time. Once there, all three men were given physicals. Tom and Stanley passed the test but Deke did not and was sent home. After passing their first physical, they were put on a train to St. Louis, Missouri where they received another physical. The next day, the 22nd, they were put on the Louisville and Nashville Railroad to Atlanta, Georgia and given instructions on how to proceed.

Tom's Travel Instructions

United States Marine Corps
Central Recruiting Division
Headquarters District of Missouri
215 Fullerton Bldg., 122 N. 7th St.
St Louis, Missouri

June 22, 1917

From: Officer in Charge.
To: Accepted Applicant Thomas L. Stewart, M.C.
Subject: Travel Orders

You will proceed this date via the Louisville and Nashville Railroad to Atlanta, Ga., where, immediately upon your arrival you will report to the Officer in Charge, Southeastern Recruiting District for further transportation to the Marine Barracks, Port Royal, S.C.

Your train schedule is as follows:

Leave St Louis, Mo. 4:09 PM
Arrive Nashville, Tenn. 2:30 AM
Leave Nashville, Tenn. 3:00 AM
Arrive Atlanta, Ga. 11:45 AM

Upon your arrival in Atlanta look for a man in uniform standing by the Marine Corps Recruiting Sign at Station. Should you fail to see him ask the way of the Station attendants and proceed to the Marine Recruiting Station, 29-1/2 Marietta Street, or if after 5:00 PM report to the Kimball Hotel, Corner Wall and Prior Streets, directly across the street from the Union Depot.

Transportation and Subsistence for the travel involved is necessary in the public service are herewith furnished you.

F. M. Fslick.

During this ride, the recruits prepared for their official examinations to determine if they could become Marines. This was a bit of disappointment for Tom and Stanley as they believed they would be training in California.[5] However, despite his disappointment, Tom was lucky enough to meet the standards for the Corps. One poor recruit was too skinny to make the weight and as Tom says in his memoir: "he ate bananas (the only food available) all the way to Atlanta where we stopped over night at the Kimball House."[6] Once they arrived in Atlanta, they were sent to Port Royal, South Carolina and examined. From there they were sent via motor boat to Paris Island, South Carolina.

Paris Island was an eight-thousand-square-acre piece of hot, insect-infected, flat bog that became the primary recruit depot and training ground for Marines who had enlisted east of the

---

5   Paris Island was supposed to be the training base for all recruits East of the Mississippi and all recruits from the West were to train in California.

6   Tom later admits that the poor recruit did manage to make the weight.

Mississippi.[7] When the Marines arrived in 1917 the island was still being constructed. It had no roads, barracks, nor latrines capable of handling the thousands of new recruits.[8] These new Marines were given physical work to strengthen their bodies that consisted of digging the latrines, trenches for pipelines, collecting shells for roads, and mixing concrete for the barracks and other works. It was a hard life but it was meant to be. As Tom says later in a letter, "the life on the island really shouldn't be called a part of the life in the service for they make it hard on recruits purposely. I suppose so they won't crab if they ever run up against anything like it on an expeditionary force or something where it can't be helped." At one point the Marines were told point blank: "Don't write home and tell your impressions till you get to the barracks as you might influence men not to enlist." Tom was assigned to the 82nd Company, Company "H", while on the island. The island was hell on earth but it is where the Marines were hardened before moving on to further training.

Letter to Folks, June 22, 1917

Wellington Hotel
St. Louis, Mo.
June 22, 1917

Dear Folks:

Got in here yesterday morning. Went right up and got examined. We both got by but they sure had me worried for a while. Pretty strict, and I have a tendency toward flat feet but they let me by on it.

We are shipped this evening at four PM to Port Royal—a whole car of us. I don't know whether we go in

---

7   James Carl Nelson, *I Will Hold: The USMC Legend Clifton B. Cates, from Belleau Wood to Victory in the Great War,* (New York: New American Library, 2016), 26.

8   Ibid, 27.

a cattle car or a Pullman. We expected to get out yesterday but they held us till today, so we got to see some of the town. Went out to the "Y" and looked up an old college friend and brother, and also chased out to some of the parks.[9]

The Marines are sure fine fellows. Both at Wichita and here they have sure treated us fine. Gentlemen and good fellows. Haven't seen anyone above top sergeant yet. Most all sergeants, and have met and talked to several who were at Vera Cruz, one who was wounded there. There were nine wounded out of a 3000 landing party. That's not bad.

Sure is a chance to enlist here. Take anything you want. Army, Navy, Marines, national guards, truck drivers, or anything, and lots of publicity.

Also went in and got pilly with a couple of bank presidents.

Well must close this. Will write when we arrive at Port Royal. Will get our uniforms and equipment there; and no other clothes allowed in the barracks till training is over. They are rushing them thru and we probably will be there but six weeks.

Will send you an address as soon as we get there. Imagine U.S.M.C., Port Royal, S.C. will reach us all right tho.

Lots of love,
TOM.

---

9   The "Y" referring to the YMCA.

Letter to Folks, June 26, 1917

At Quarantine Station
Port Royal, S.C.

Dear Folks,

Well we have arrived and we are awaiting examination. They say they give some examination here, but I guess we can get by all right.

Well I guess I'd better start and tell about the trip. The first thing of interest after we left Wichita was the oil well district. We passed right thru the Augusta fields; and the wells are thicker than windmills in Spearville. One in every back yard and sometimes two or three.

We passed thru the Ozarks in the night so didn't get to see much there. We were held over in St. Louis, so looked around a bit. Also went out and visited a college fraternity brother. We left there on a limited train. Had nearly 30 fellows, all a pretty good sort. Of course a couple of rowdies which we had to endure.

I was a little disappointed in the Mississippi, also in the Ohio River. Didn't quite come up to my expectations. We went thru a corner of Indiana—Evansville the stop there. Then thru Kentucky and Tennessee. It was daylight when we crossed the Cumberland Mts. and we sure saw some pretty country. Began to run into some pines from there on, but different from the Colorado pines.

Then we went on into Georgia; they are thicker and are largely pine there also. We went down a little way into Alabama, stopped at Stevenson. Also stopped at Chattanooga and saw the Little General, the principal actor in Andrews famous raid. We went over the same route but from the opposite direction. Also saw Big

Shanty, (Kansan now) where the locomotive was stolen and the raid began.[10]

The soil in Georgia is as red as the reddest face brick you ever saw and is of claylike consistency. From the Cumberlands to Atlanta is mostly a corn country and a little cotton as you near Atlanta.

Little old huts and negroes everywhere; very few whites except in the towns, and there they are outnumbered.

Atlanta is a pretty nice town. Crooked as can be tho. A terrible lot of niggers; and the whites that are here have the money. The girls are pretty as pictures.

Sure didn't like St. Louis. It is the dirtiest hole I ever struck and wet. About ten times as bad as Denver when I was there, and it was wide open then.

There are about 20,000 soldiers at Atlanta and almost every other white person is a soldier. There will be some 80,000 later, as the cantonment will be there.

Georgia and S. Carolina are both bone dry without the bone dry however, as there seems to be plenty of ways of getting it.

The soil gets better as we go to S.C. Also gets low. When there is a stream there are semi swamps for about a mile around it. There are southern pines all along after you get into S.C., pretty heavily wooded.

We got on a jerk water from Augusta on and got to the end of the line about seven thirty last night. Shipped in a boat and started out again. We are on an island about three miles from the mainland. It does not seem like it tho, for we haven't seen the sea, tho the lagoons have more water in them than any I have ever seen.

The Atlantic fleet, or a part of it, is over at Charleston not far from here.

---

10 I believe he means that Big Shanty is now called Kennesaw not Kansan.

Our work has not yet begun, tho we had "submarine drill" this AM. We will be examined this PM or tomorrow and vaccinated. Then sworn in and given equipment. We can't keep a thing so I guess I'll send mine home. We are in quarantine now and not at the barracks. It will be some three weeks before we get there. Here is where we get our labor and hardships. Everything is new; just put up over night. One of the N.C.O. said that if we went on an expedition, we wouldn't see any more hardships than we will here the next few weeks. However it doesn't look so bad and when it's over it's smooth sailing and a good time.

There is no censorship of mail as yet and every one is anxious for there not to be, and to that end we are advised not to tell very much about anything here. So don't repeat anything except that I'm here working hard and having a good time.

We have no butter nor condiments and only two things to eat usually, and coffee, but plenty of whatever there is.

Ever since five thirty there has been a constant volley over on the range. About three companies, they are almost thru their "hell" and about ready to go to the barracks. There are over 6500 men on the island now, recruits and old men.

Whenever anyone has time, be sure to write. I don't have any other address than U.S.M.C., Port Royal S.C. We move about from one camp to another so that we can't give a real definite one but guess they will find us eventually.

Must close this now. Ink gave out so I had to use pencil. Please excuse.

Lots of love,
TOM.

Would give a little for a freshwater bath. This stuff leaves you so sticky.

Letter to Viv, June 27, 1917

Port Royal, S.C.
Quarantine Station.
Wednesday.

Dear Viv:

Well we got our uniforms today. There has sure been
enough red tape about it. Took all day yesterday to be
examined. Sure learn to be patient standing in line under
a tropical sun with nothing on but a towel. They wear
anything—that is up till the time they get their uniforms.
From a towel on up. It is hot as the deuce until you get in
the shade, then as cool as you could wish for. Have ocean
breeze all right and tide but that's all the ocean we've seen
or are likely to see for weeks. We are all at quarantine
station. Have all been vaccinated and are in quarantine
right as there is one case of small pox.

Ordinarily we would go "over the fence" in a day or two.
As it is no one knows, so address me there until further
notice as it will follow us anyway. (Co. 82).

I sent my suitcase to dad and necessarily had to send
it collect (unless U.S. pays—nothing was said). Now I
couldn't shut it very well and couldn't get a strap, but I
put my address inside and everything and valued it at $35
so if it doesn't arrive in a reasonable time, set them after it
as I can't from here. It is sent Southern Express.

My suit I think you can wear very well. It needs a good
cleaning and pressing. You and dad divide up. I don't want
anything and when I come out I'll want to buy new ones
anyway. Also at Patchens my trunk is packed except as:
two overcoats in the closet—one a piece, a couple of suits
also in closet, a tennis racket and a gun. In the bottom
of the trunk is all dirty clothes. They ought to be taken
out and washed and used. Also use any clothes in the top
trays. The rest leave in those trays. Whenever anyone goes

to Spearville better check my trunk home on their ticket. The key to it is in top left dresser drawer. I enclose key to suitcase. There are two Phi Delta Theta pins in my coat pocket. Ward wore one. Put them in a safe place — say in with some other stuff like that in upper right hand tray of trunk. Also Masonic lapel button on coat.

Ross promised to deposit $4.00 per month to dad's credit at the First National for room rent.

Beginning today our hell begins. So if I shouldn't write too frequently don't worry. I'll be all right only working 10 to 16 hours every day. It won't be so bad when we get to the barracks as everything is fixed up fine over there, but here — to do what they said — "Don't write home and tell your impressions till you get to the barracks as you might influence men not to enlist" and, they say it's pretty fine over there. It will have to be to make up for this. But we'll all live thru it and probably be better off.

Saw a steamer today quite a ways out-only could make out the form.

We will get our shots in the arm in a few days. Typhoid, prophylaxis, three shots at intervals of several days. There are a few that faint away every time. Some did when they were vaccinated. It made me sick at my stomach. The grub nearly does that tho. They say its better tho as they go on. We had a bunch of 90 sworn in today and filled in two companies. Ours (82) is not quite full yet. Will be tomorrow.

Must close this now.
Love,
TOM

If you are not at home send this on and let them read it.

Excerpt from Tom's Memoir

Next day train took us to Port Royal, S. C. where an open motor boat took us to Paris Island. Supper time came and we were served a plate of macaroni—no cheese no bread no nothing. It was a big disappointment.

Letter to Folks, July 4, 1917

Paris Island, S. C.

Dear Folks,

This is a holiday. This day and Christmas are the only ones the soldiers get. We have sure had a fair sample so far of a soldier's life.

Yesterday we dug trenches all day for a double purpose I suppose. Anyway it was for a pipeline. Dug in marsh bog and in rock and shell and in the ordinary soil here which was fine—a clay sand and easy to dig.

This morning we had a field meet among the five drill companies in camp. We had a regular meal today too. Chicken, mashed potatoes, dressing, gravy, lemonade, cucumbers, bananas and oranges. Right after dinner, we were just thinking what a good meal we had had and the Captain called for everybody at the dock. New moon last night and an awfully high tide. It began to go out to a correspondingly unusual low level this noon and nearly dumped a gravel barge. He set us to work unloading the barge and it immediately set in and rained to beat the deuce and everyone got soaked to the bone. Just now got my clothes off and a shower.

I haven't gotten a letter yet but suppose it's the rotten mail. Neither Stan nor I have heard from anyone except I had a letter from Mrs. Patchen. No one gets any mail. They sure are rotten in taking care of it.

We get away from here this week and our work starts in earnest. We have about the best company commander in camp and have been pretty lucky so far.

Must close this now.

Love,
TOM

Letter to Folks, July 24, 1917

Paris Island,

Dear Folks:

I got quite a gob of mail today. Got letter from Viv, also from Helen and mama and tonight one from uncle Harry and a package from Miss Brazell, a cousin of Helen Lynch so I could scarcely complain today.

Well we finally got moved into the new barracks today. Made our march of about five miles with our packs and rifles. One fine hot day with the wind in our backs which made it hot as the devil. But we came thru in a lot better shape than the march over to the camp.

We got here about two thirty and found some real live shower baths which we hit the first thing. Then ate at four thirty, and washed our clothes after supper.

The barracks here are the same as at the quarantine camp but we have sanitary cots instead of the army cots, and we have mattresses and pillows; and about the same amount of drill and work as before. I am beginning to get a little used to it now and think this will be all right here.

I wish I could have gotten a picture of the maneuver camp before we left, to send you, for it is really a pretty place right in camp. We will be here in this camp about six or seven weeks it is supposed. But we really can't tell anything about it. Only judge from the ones ahead of us.

Aunt Maud sent me this stationary today, which I sure appreciated. I guess boys have a reputation for not writing.

I have kept pretty well so far except for a few days off feed or something. Haven't been on the sick list yet and I am truly thankful, for the so-called medical attention is nix. All they know is iodine and salts and that is all you get.

I am glad Granny is getting along so fine. I hope the heat won't be too hard on her. Harry seemed to be thinking I was having a hard time of it. I didn't mean to leave that impression. We are working hard but nobody has hurt himself as far as I know. I sure have not.

I have had to stop writing about a half dozen times. I started this yesterday.

We worked today—this is noon now. Have been working in concrete. I have pushed a wheelbarrow all morning; I think it's about the pick job. Hard, but don't have to work too fast.

Since we have gotten over here the eats have been almost civilized. Tastes more like outside meals. Have plates and knife, fork and spoon, too. Had beef, mashed spuds & gravy today also watermelon. Have had butter over here too, for the first time. We have watermelon once in a while but they won't allow us to buy them. They have a canteen here where they sell most anything, but there is such a mob of men always that you can't buy anything.

Well must close this now. Get it out of your head that I am sick or anything for I'm feelin' fine, only working hard.

Tell Viv, tho' to stay out. I say that not because I don't like it or think it would be too hard for him, but they will need men later on, say a year from now, as badly as they do now. They won't shut off volunteering, don't worry. At least not in the Marines. The Marines won't have a drafted man on the roll, also they have no negroes and never will have. I'm not trying to place the two in the same class tho.

Please notice if I got drafted. A lot of the fellows are finding out and it's interesting to know. Will be in the Spearville News I guess.

Well must close this now and try to write a few others. Ross spoke about my dress suit. It hangs in the closet over at Granny's; also a pair of white serge pants. I have a pair of 12-inch high top boots over there some place, too, that are good. I'd like to keep it all together if you can find them. If anybody can wear them, go ahead. Sure Helen, go ahead and wear that coat and anything else you want.

It was reported or rather rumored this morning that we would be in France the first of Sept. You can hear anything like that here tho. I think by Oct. 1st tho anyway.

Well, must close this now,

Lots of love,
TOM

Bathrobe in my room—never mind it. It is almost worn out anyway.

Letter to Helen, August 3, 1917

Paris Island, S. C.

Dear Helen:

I got your letter yesterday evening. We are drilling now in the evening and usually just get our mail in time to read it before dark.

We are working on skirmish drill now and bayonet exercise with a little double time every morning before breakfast to give us an appetite. We are all getting corns on our elbows and stomachs from walking on them so much. Have also to learn to fall flat on the dead run with a rifle in our hands.

We drew another detail today, making two this week.
General police duty. But that is not as romantic as it
sounds. Consists of galley incinerator and clean up work.

It sure rained last night. May cool it off some for awhile,
I hope so. Is cloudy today anyway. Storm came up when
we were out on the parade ground and we got double all
the way in.

Had officers review yesterday morning and we were
color company. I suppose we made asses of ourselves,
we always do, so our commander tells us. I'd like to see
ourselves some times anyway. It sure must make a trainer
sore.

Yes. I knew about Paul.[11] I had thought of going into
the signal branch of the M. C. but it means 10 to 20 more
weeks on the island and I couldn't stand that. Besides
every Marine has to have a good deal of that; supposed to
be able to send and to receive. In the army only the Signal
Corps does.

I am going to send my watch home as soon as I can get
a box to pack it in. I sure did a fool trick. We have to wash
a complete outfit every day and the other day I put my
trousers in to soak and forgot to take out my watch. Take
it to a good jeweler when it comes and have it cleaned for
me and you or anyone else can use it till I need it again. It
is really more bother than use to me. I wish I had sent it
home at first. I had a notion to.

Yes, the kodak came thru fine and was exactly what I
wanted. I expected to pay for it tho and sure appreciate it.

I'm getting The News direct now. Rosa sends it to
Spearville Sammies.

Tell Dorothy when you write to look around over at
granny's and get the Saturday Evening Post for June 30th

---

11 Paul is Tom's cousin: Paul Irwin.

and send it to me. I wanted it especially and it was the one they missed when they sent that other bunch.

Had better close this for we are about to fall out for work.

Lots of love,
TOM.

Letter to Folks, August 10, 1917

Paris Island, S. C.

Dear Folks:

Got a letter from mama a few days ago, also one from dad last night enclosing papers. Muchas gratias. See southern papers here once in awhile but a person doesn't get interested in them if he doesn't see them regularly. I also had a letter from Aunt Minnie last night. It is good of her to write me.

I'll answer questions first. I am not keeping a diary but will have a kodak record if I can. We use Springfield rifles, 30 caliber, high power. They weigh 8 ½ pounds. Will carry five miles or more and have sight gauge to 2700 yards. That is it carries true to 2700 yards. There are five sights, but we use but two. The battle sight and the peep sight.

Battle sight is fixed at 530 yards & we have to estimate the distance, ourselves, on the target higher or lower when at closer or further range. We shoot rapid fire, battle sight, at 200, 300 and 500 yards; and slow fire at 300, 500, and 600 yards. Takes keen shooting to crack a 20 inch bull's eye at 600 yards, or an 8 inch one at 300 yards.

In rapid fire we have a silhouette figure to represent head and shoulders of a man same size.

The Allies use the Enfield rifle. Those of us who go to France will probably get one of them because of the ammunition being easier to get. The Springfield, tho, is

the best rifle, altho the Enfield is simpler, they say. We do
not carry any ammunition and are not allowed to have any.
On the range they give us just what we are to shoot right
at the time.

We usually shoot about forty or sixty rounds a day. We
will get some practice with revolvers but are not issued
any. They use Colt .45.

We haven't gotten the rest of our equipment. It
will consist of a bayonet, cartridge belt, and knapsack.
Are supposed to carry in knapsack one change of
clothing—everything from bottom up—all toilet
articles, and two days rations. Also a poncho and later
on trenching tools and one or two blankets, according to
weather.

We have two piece underwear. Nainsook drawer and
balbriggon shirts with quarter sleeves. They furnish a
heavier one for winter.

At present we keep all our clothes under our mattress,
and toilet and other articles in our bucket under our bunk.
(14 in size) Nothing is allowed to be seen. Bunk is made
up thus:

Our names are on the blankets and they are folded over
the top fold of mattress so that the name shows in front.

We never get anything fresh except sometimes on
Sundays, either watermelon or oranges for dessert. There
are stores in the main barracks, but the only time we can
get there is when marching thru and we can't fall out.

From what we hear when we get to Va. We may be able
to get to Washington over Sunday sometimes. It is only 30
miles. If so, you may be sure I'll buy a real meal if it costs
my month's pay. We get no oysters but plenty of oyster
shells. They make roads out of them and the rookies carry
them in. We've had enough of that to make us sick at
sight of oyster shell.

That was all right on the furniture. We paid $7.50 apiece, and it's all as good as new. The dresser was mine really for Tom gave the old thing to Ross and me but I did the work and paid for everything that went into it, to make it a real dresser.

There is a rifle and a tennis racket there which can go in Bess room, I guess. My pennants and pictures are on wall. They can stay unless Mrs. P. wants them down. If so, put them in my trunk if you think about it. Moths will eat them in Bess room.

No, I suppose I wouldn't have had to go, but then I wouldn't have wanted to stay, either, so it's just as well I went when I did.

From what the paper said I understood there would be none taken from Ford County. That makes a pretty good showing.

Tell Viv I got his letter and will answer soon. Must close this,

Lots of love,
TOM

Letter to Folks, August 15, 1917

Paris Island, S. C.
Sunday

Dear Folks:

Haven't anything very interesting to write since last time. We are still getting lots of work. Besides that this morning the "Corp" got sore at us on one of his own beefs and gave us drill on the double for about a half an hour.

We got a pretty decent feed today. Pork chops and apple sauce. A pretty poor imitation of what it would have been at home but it was good in comparison. I have almost turned vegetarian since coming in here. I have seen too much of the meat before it is cooked.

I got the box of candy and sure was tickled and surprised, you can be sure I was thankful for it. Stan got a box the same day so we had a day of rejoicing.

We are getting our mail all right now. This is not a bad place to be. The chief objection is that there is no place to take a decent bath and as we are working every day, I rather hate that.

We are getting up at five now, drilling a couple of hours before breakfast, then work the rest of the day. Have chow at five so we knock off work at four and have a little time to ourselves on evenings that we don't have to wash clothes.

"Our men may have time for study" but not on this island; there is a lot of time between ten PM and five AM with nothing to do but sleep. I will sure be glad when we get off but I guess they all go thru it. Don't fool yourself.

I wish we would get some vegetables and fresh fruit or even fish. We get beans, rice, stew; grits; and beans and rice in regular rotation. Coffee for breakfast, water for dinner and ice tea for supper, heavy on the ice.

Stanley and I are bunking together so far. Did I tell you we had seen Bleger from Spearville. He is ahead of us and has gone on.

The key to the Bess room is in the dresser drawer in my room, also trunk key. Any key will unlock Bess room if you can't find it.

Don't worry about vaccination. It is all O. K. Never bothered any; the typhoid vacillis left a sore arm for a day, that's all.

Mighty glad to get letters from Dorothy, Lois, Vera, Helen, and everybody else. Some were delayed two weeks or more, but they are coming in now in about four days from home.

We are now the senior company here. Eight companies went out today and two more came in from quarantine. Suppose we won't get out till next Sunday now. That seems to be the day for moving troops from this place.

We have no bed bugs here, that is one advantage over the barracks. Stan had a letter from Deac; said since he came back he had answered 100 questions, knocked five men down, and almost perpetrated one murder; that he and Red Alkire—Viv can tell you who he is—were the only ones rejected yet.

Gee, it sure must be hot there. It gets pretty hot here but nights are always cool and breeze cool whenever we have it.

Too bad so many glass were broken. Has Taylor enlisted or merely getting footloose for the draft?

What is the Big Store going to do when Ross leaves? I see he joined the Wichita battery company.

Don't you think Viv had better hold down a job at the greenhouse till spring, or is there enough in it to make it interesting for him? I don't think he ought to go for a year yet anyway.

The men here are all old timers and have seen at least one enlistment. They rather have a little contempt for the army, not out and out; but you can see it. Almost open tho for the militia. And the navy, I don't exactly know. Everyone says the jackies are afraid of them.[12]

We don't get anything to read. If anyone wants the Post, write in and have the address changed to Larned; the Spearville folks never read it anyway. It comes to T. A. Stewart by the way. I can't have it come to me because I'd waste too much postage having it changed.

I think the navy is full, they reported it so at St. Louis. Viv might join and wait till they call him, but I think he'd

---

12 "Jackies" is a slang term for sailors.

better wait. There's no use to be in a hurry and it's sure no snap now and not all sunshine. I have no doubt he'd get in all right in either. The Navy and Marines are both lots stricter than the army. The men the Marines turn down are sent right over to the army. Of course they don't have to go into the army if they don't want to.

Well I must close this now and write to the folks at Spearville.

Lots of love to everyone,
TOM.

Letter to Viv, August 16, 1917

Paris Island, S. C.

Dear Viv:

Have been hitting the old ball pretty steadily this week but the bull's eye not so often.

We changed shifts this week and now have the late shift. Go out at ten thirty, in again at two thirty and back at three thirty 'til seven thirty. It is usually pretty dusky when we stop shooting. Have been shooting rapid fire these last few days. I have fallen off considerable but have hopes of bringing it up again. Have to make 42 on five ranges and 43 on the other to get expert. My coach says he is going to make an expert out of me and I sure hope he does.

The right senior companies shoot for record today and tomorrow so I don't suppose we will get to shoot much; but after that we'll get 50 to 100 rounds a day, and then a week from today shoot for record, so pray for a bright day and no wind. The windage is the most uncertain part of it as you have to estimate the velocity of it, then the rest is easy.

Am stiff all over today; guess will come out of it before we shoot again. Just stopped there and ran out and took some pictures of the parade this morning.

This morning shift has brought us a lot of extra work up to today. Get up at six instead of four fifteen, but then instead of reading or using that time for ourselves, we have to work. Today tho we missed for a wonder.

The company next door to us 83rd got called up for office hours. They had inspection yesterday and their bunks were not properly made up. They will get about 20 hours extra duty. We escaped only because we had our door locked and were all out on the range. We missed the fire call too, by not getting in early. I hope they don't have another. That is the first one since we have been here. It means double time with buckets about the length of the camp.

We got our lockers yesterday. Big old box to put your clothes and toilet articles in. Have to keep them on your bunk in day time and under at night. It is more bother than it's worth.

There is a chance of getting a furlough after we go to Quantico. Ten days and traveling time. If I can find out about rates I may make use of it. The Chicago and also St. Louis bunch will have special cars at least so that it will cost about $5.00 from Washington to either of those two points. However I'll let you all know when I can find out more definite information.

The ones who live in the south here go from here and northern men from Quantico.

If I should make expert, I can stay here and coach if I want to. I'll wait till I make it however before deciding anything like that.

Bleger made marksman; just missed sharpshooter by five points. He got thru last Thursday and is in at the Main now.

Stan and I and about fifty others got leave and went over to Port Royal Tuesday night and went to lodge. Seemed good to be in the U. S. A. again and was quite a treat to get off the island and do as you please once.

Sure lots of niggers there and they sure put on the comedy just like you read about in books.

Well must close this and get ready to go out.

Yours,
TOM

Is Lois home yet? Had a letter from her. She expected to leave the fifteenth.

Letter to Folks, August 19, 1917

Paris Island, S. C.

Dear Folks:

Nothing much doing this week; same old grind out on the rifle range. We put in our share of the time behind the butts at work and haven't shot very much yet. Monday, Tuesday, and Wednesday we will get about 60 rounds or more each, and then Thursday and Friday we shoot for record. Makes very little real practice—not half what they used to get.

There was a scrap this week about miss marking targets and several fellows got summary court martial; so from now on, for a while at least, we may be sure that we really did shoot whatever we get, for the new fellows are scared to death.

I haven't much hopes any more for anything but marksman but you never can tell. My coach says he's going to make an expert out of me, here's hoping he does. We haven't shot for several days on account of record shooting of senior companies.

Bleger was over here last night. He expects to leave for Quantico tomorrow. They are forming the sixth and seventh regiments for duty in France supposedly. We will doubtless be formed in the seventh but know nothing for certain of course.

Our corporal was made a sergeant the other day and acting jack a corporal; they go fast in war times, but they are hard; if you can't deliver the goods they kick you out just as quickly.

Quite nice to read about the meals the Topeka guardsmen get — as in Topeka Capital. They are living on the fat of the land.

We have coffee for breakfast, water for dinner, and ice tea for supper invariably. The water is all salt filtered once and is not the best tasting in the world. On Sundays we have mashed spuds and beef or pork roast and gravy and an orange. Other days we have for breakfast, never more than two things; bacon and oatmeal, or grits and hot dog, or beans alone. About once a week have oleo. This morning, being Sunday, had eggs, two, one of mine was spoiled; and pancakes and syrup, two cakes; first time anything like that has ever happened.

For dinners we have beans, and rice in some form or other usually, maybe a boiled spud. Three things usually including dessert which is ordinarily rice pudding or bread pudding. If we have gravy that counts as one article. Nobody ever kicks tho on the grub as long as there is enough, but when there isn't there is a squeal.

We had all our bunks out this morning for an airing. Just got thru putting them away as it looks quite rainy. The rainy season won't begin in earnest I guess till we are away from here. Here's hoping anyway. Every change of the moon tho it rains for a day or two; then we walk in water to the range for a day and the next day go up to our

ankles in dust and sand again. The mud never is deep but
is certainly dirty.

Got liberty last Tuesday night and went over to Port
Royal to lodge. About six men in civilians and a house full
of khaki. Managed to get in all O. K. My first attempt at a
foreign lodge.

Port Royal is a rotten sleepy typical southern town.
About four fourths negroes. It is just a switch, really
established for the Barracks. They have been here only
about three years.

It was also the first time I had been inside the Barracks.
It is nice in there. They have a big brick theatre and
gymnasium, also barracks of same and one nice street of
officers' homes, and the rest tent streets, power plant and
docks and—most important—the "brig" the naval prison,
which scares us all, as the guard house as well.

Two men from our company got the "brig" for the target
business. Thirty days and a fine I think and of course a
mark against their record.

I am writing this at the "Y." It is a large frame building
about 40' X 100' with benches and writing desks running
the length of it on each side. They also have a little
reading matter here and free paper, pen and ink. Have
a pool table but it must be sacred, haven't seen anyone
using it. Have checkers and chess boards also.

They tell us that the French are firing on the Sammies
in trenches to get them used to fire.[13] Rifle fire and not to
hit of course, only to come close.

Did you ever get the box I sent home? I had to give up
insuring it.

That is sure the deuce about the hail. Makes a lot of
extra work I suppose.

---

13 "Sammies" is slang of the time for American soldiers.

Would like to see the Bank building at Spearville. Know it will be good looking. Guess they are not yet in it are they? Had a letter from W. Pine other day; he said nothing about it.[14]

The proposition of paying out on M.W.A. policies was to be taken up at the Head Camp this July. What did they do? If they are not paying wish you would have my insurance dropped. They pay it at the bank. But there's no use paying it if it's no good; and I can pick it up again if I want to afterwards. Look in August M.W.A. paper. It will tell if they are going to pay. There is a plan on foot for the government to guarantee the extra mortality loss to the companies; don't know whether that has gone thru or not.

I knew that Mr. B. was leaving the Big Store and supposed probably Tom would take his place. Maybe a good thing he didn't get accepted, certainly good for Mrs. W.[15] Makes a nice job for him but he'll have his hands full I imagine.

Too bad Mrs. P. is having such a hard time of it. I had a letter from her this week and judged she was working pretty hard. If she could find some boy who would take care of furnace and things for his board or a part of it, it wouldn't be so bad.

Suppose Lois will be home by now. Every body standing on their heads, too, I bet. What town in Missouri is Drury or is it in Mo.?

If I can get a ten day leave with traveling time, after we get to Quantico—next month some time—I may make use of it, if it is true about 1cent rates on Penn. Lines; could come into St. Louis on that and then on out. They

---

14 W. Pine is Will Pine.

15 Tom Westmacott is who is referenced as not being accepted when the boys applied for officer's training.

may stop the furloughs before then, tho. We never know from one day to another what we'll have or anything.

Well I must close this and get it in the mail from the "Y" here.

Lots of love to everybody,
TOM

Muster Rolls, August 24, 1917

Tom qualifies as Marksman.

Letter to Folks, August 29, 1917

Paris Island, S. C.

Dear Folks:

Got Vera's letter and mama's yesterday. Guess there was some jubilee when Lois got there; wish I had been there. Will be a house-full when Bob and Do get there. Bet you all had a good time Sunday up at Spearville. Suppose the Chat. is good. Is it awfully hot there now?

Speaking of soldiers not having uniforms; a couple of weeks ago they sent a bunch over the fence with only leggings and pajamas. No nothing almost. Are in better shape now. Have shut down on them now. The quarantine Camp and Maneuver grounds have been under quarantine for over two weeks for spinal meningitis. We've heard all kinds of tales but the only thing is to believe none of them. We simply know they are quarantined. A lot of their N.C.O.S. like to spread stuff around to the recruits and watch them swallow it.

Yes, they give a bar medal for marksman; don't know when we'll get it. Maybe not till end of war. They take the big men for ship duty, have to be a certain height and weight. I don't suppose I'd make it.

Yes, we spent half our time marking targets. No they weren't strict but some of the fellows gave them too much and of course the officers use field glasses on the targets record day and they caught a few of them. If a shot comes as near as a half inch from the bull's eye, they get a bull usually, but these kids would give a five on a complete miss, sometimes. It made it pretty hard on us for the kids back there for us were scared to death and marked us close as the deuce. We get to shoot once a year, if we are not too far away from a range. The Corps has only this one and one at Quantanomo Bay, Cuba. This is the best in U.S.A. except possibly at Plattsburg, N. Y.

I haven't finished that roll of films yet. I'm sending you a negative tho. Have six made off it when you can—no hurry.

So they have a preacher at Spearville again now. Is he to Weyand's liking?

I got a dandy comfort kit from the S. Red Cross. Sure had everything almost. The one thing that looked good to me was mentholatum. Can't buy it here.

We are now on our ten days of hard labor, supposed to be 16 hours. Did Monday all right, unloading lumber and brick.

Yesterday we went over and drew some equipment and clothes. It rained and we had to stand out in it of course. They have no respect at all for us privates. We drew our cartridge belts and bayonets. They sure are wicked old steak knives and sharp. I'll be scared of my own rifle with it on. They are hard to keep from rusting, of course, as everything we have almost is. Have to keep them brighter than said new dollar.

Today we were over at Main mixing concrete and quit at seven because the engine broke down. We'd be working yet I guess but for that. tomorrow we go in the mess halls.

We expect to get out of here Monday or a week from Monday at the latest.

I had to stop there and go sign the payroll; of course I hated to do it. Now I've got to clean up my rifle and go take a bath and go to bed. Have a rule that no one goes to bed without a bath just for protection against some of the dirty squad. I get me one every morning about five thirty and there's no hot water, then at night and during the day if we get a chance.

It rained this morning like the deuce but we "Marines" hardly ever care for that. Was about two inches of water all over the road and we had to make it into the Main Barracks and back twice. One thing as a usual thing it doesn't get muddy but water stands on top.

Well must close this.

Lots of love,
TOM

Letter to Folks, September 3, 1917

Paris Island, S. C.

Dear Folks:

This seems more like the 3rd of July than Sept. It has been hot enough for summer but otherwise it doesn't seem to have been any summer at all. We seem to be celebrating Labor Day today; had inspection at eight o'clock and haven't done anything since. I was lucky enough to have a clean rifle, so got out of extra duty.

Our company plays another game of ball today. We are champions of the island—some 60 or 70 companies and if we win they may go over to Beaufort to play.

We sure deserved our lay off today. Worked all last week. The company drilled one day but I was detailed in mess hall so had to work. Had two days of Port Royal; that means from seven to nine always and sometimes later. Unloaded brick, lumber and gravel on barges, brought them over and unloaded them. One day in at the Main mixing concrete and one day drawing clothes and equipment, two in mess halls.

We are hoping to get out of here next week. A bunch leave tomorrow for Quantico, Norfolk, and New Orleans. They took up to the 81st company and we will now be the next to leave. The 81st, 82nd, 83rd will all be mustered into one company, making full strength of about 200 men.

We had quite a feed this noon. Beef roast, mashed spuds and gravy, oleo, canned corn and grape juice to drink—first time anything like that has happened and had lots of it, also oranges.

Was over at the Y.M.C.A. last night for the services. Had a real good talk. They are furnishing everything for the amusement of the men, footballs, handballs, baseball paraphernalia, quots etc., checkers, chess, and pool inside. Are organizing French classes in the different companies.

When we first came over here to the new barracks, the senior company was the 30th. They have gone and day after tomorrow we will be senior to but one, and a new thirty company is over here. About twenty companies at the maneuver grounds and quarantine station. The big trouble is to get equipment. Some companies just got their rifles the other day and have been here a month. Will double up their work for awhile no doubt, now learning the manual of arms. We hear that at Quantico they are teaching the army manual; ours are a little different in a few details, but will not be hard to change, I suppose.

Well must close this. I am trying to write in the bunk house and there is getting to be too much of a rough house.

Lots of love,
TOM

Letter to Helen, September 7, 1917

Paris Island, S. C.

Dear Helen:

Got your letter a couple of nights ago but this is the first chance for an answer. They have very little respect for our time after supper, even if they want it.

That day we were over on the U.S.A. and unloaded two cars of bricks, one of lumber and one of implements, and after supper loaded and unloaded a car of lumber on trucks from the docks to the H.D. over on this side. When we got in, it was quarter to ten which made it nice for us of course.

Have drilled since then and on drill days it is not so strenuous; today drilled and parade for about three hours, then this evening two hours work on parade grounds.

This afternoon played a game of ball, our company against the post team, which beat them 15 to 1 and rather took them back. Their first defeat. Still hope to go to Savannah but doubt if they will get to.

We still hope to get out of here Tuesday but may get held over for a couple of weeks on account of lengthening it to a twelve week schedule. Have started a French class in the company and I am brushing up. I had a year of it but it is surprising how much a person forgets when he is not using it. It's three years since I had it.

I wrote Viv a letter the other day. I wish he would go to school too. There is no need of him in the service and it is sure no place for character molding. I can say that without casting any reflections on it in the least, but for an older man, at least of age I should say, for then a person relies more upon his own judgment of things and is not so easily led: rather influenced is the word I guess.

Was talking to a sergeant-major this evening who is a square and compass man and we are going over to lodge again Tuesday.

No really that cake was fine. No danger of anything drying out here and it wasn't broken up either.

Doubt if I get a furlough. Will get one Christmas if I am in the U.S.A. Don't know if we get shipped with the next bunch or not. If not have heard that no more Marines go till Jan 1.

Well must close this now. Guess you'll get it all right at school. Suppose there'll be hundreds of khaki men to all the college affairs this year.

Lots of love,
TOM

Excerpt from Tom's Memoir

Our company had won the Island baseball championship and got to go to Savannah to play an Army team. Anyone who had the money could go as a spectator. Stanley and I did not go. At this juncture, orders came through for 200 men for Quantico, Va. for training for overseas. The ball team and rooters missed out as we were gone when they got back.

CHAPTER TWO
QUANTICO

AFTER TRAINING for close to three months, Tom and Stanley were moved to Quantico, Virginia on September 11, 1917.[16] Outside the town of Quantico was a six-thousand-acre camp built as another training ground.[17] It was here that the Marines received their combat training for the conditions they would face in Europe. Trench warfare became the standard exercise. In the mountains around Quantico, practice trenches and barbed wire entanglements served as their school. The Marines were trained by Canadian officers, English officers, and Scottish officers on the hell that was France. The training involved "machine gun instruction, bayonet drill, dummy hand grenades, rifle range practice, trench digging, trench warfare, combat drills, and the basic principles and fundamentals of modern warfare."[18] These were supplemented with lectures on gas by the officers. Tom says in his memoir that "after drill days, they were sent to take a dip in the Potomac but gave it up after a few weeks when the water became frigid."

It was not all training, though. The Marines had the opportunity to take trips into Washington D.C. on the weekends, since it was not too far. Tom and Stanley took these trips as often as they could. Being close to the city gave the Marines a way of reconnecting with civilian life. They attended dances and gatherings

---

16 U.S. Marine Corps Muster Rolls: 1893-1958. Microfilm Publication T977, 460 rolls, Records of the U.S. Marine Corps, Record Group 127, National Archives in Washington D.C.

17 Nelson, *I Will Hold*, 29.

18 United States Marine Corps, *History of the 96ᵗʰ Company, 6ᵗʰ Marine Regiment in World War I*, (Washington DC: U.S. Marine Corps, 1967), 49.

hosted for Masons or at the YMCA or caught a show downtown. Some men also had the good fortune to be invited by locals for dinner and nights out on the town. It was a stark contrast between the war and their training and the life of the American public.

It was also at Quantico that the Marines were assigned into companies, battalions, and regiments. Tom was assigned to the 96th Company which had been organized on August 28, 1917.[19] Tom mentions in his memoir that they trained "with regular Marine officers now and our own kitchen and good eats." The Marines trained at Quantico for almost four months before being shipped out to France.

Letter to Folks, September 15, 1917

Quantico, Va.

Dear Folks:

Haven't gotten any mail yet since we've been up here but guess will soon begin to get it. Sure is soft here along side of P.I. (Paris Island)

Haven't gotten up a sweat here yet. Drilled two days tho and learned something all right. Yesterday part of the company was on guard and the rest of us did police duty. That is just work, not cop duty up town or anything like that. It started to rain last night and of course I was on a work detail and got wet and today it's still raining by jerks and pretty darn chilly.

We had clothes and quarters inspection this AM and a little general police duty and that's all until Monday morning. I hope it clears up tomorrow. I thot some of going to Washington today but decided to wait till next week, if at all on account of the weather.

---

19 Ibid.

There is one thing I want. Get a silk fish line at one of your hardware stores and take and braid me a cord—either three or four strand—about the size of a chalk line and about 40 inches long. I want it for a gun pull thru. Make it no bigger than a chalk line or it won't drop thru easy. If you can buy one that size all right—no need to braid it. I want it silk tho for the strength of it. We have no ram rods and I don't want to break my string and leave a rag stick in it, and my string is getting worn out.

Was up in the mountains about a mile on a truck detail yesterday, to the trenches. They have everything up there—barbwire entanglements and all. It is sure pretty up there tho, all kinds of trees and so one.

We loaded four trucks and two ambulances yesterday to go to France. The first battalion leaves tomorrow. Floyd Bleger is in it. We will be the next to go. They go via Philadelphia and England. Of course we don't even know we are going to France, but every one says so and it's a good supposition.

There are a bunch of non-coms in this company who were at St. Louis recruiting office when we went thru last June. Quite a coincidence, n'est il pas?

Must close this now for chow.

Love,
TOM

96th Co., 6th Reg.
Quantico, Va.

Letter to Helen, September 29, 1917

Quantico, Va.

Dear Helen:

Got your letter the other day and was quite tickled to hear from you, and tickled to hear of your taking office.

Is Viv going to start in at K.S.A.C.?[20] I wrote to him and did what I could but don't know what effect it may have had if any. If he only knew what they both are, he'd beat it off to college; for now at least. There'll be plenty of time for something like this later on if need be and in the meantime he can get a taste of it in college. For you know this is a job you can't quit because you get sore at the boss or anything.

It is really a fairly decent life as we have it now and of course the life on the island really shouldn't be called a part of the life in the service for they make it hard on recruits purposely. I suppose so they won't crab if they ever run up against anything like it on an expeditionary force or something where it can't be helped.

We have more water now and I even got me a hot bath the other night. There are heaters in all the bath houses but only a few are allowed to use them for some unknown reason.

We were up in the trenches one day this week and had a little warfare. Sent in an attacking force with bayonet and bombs, to see how many men would get "killed" in taking the trench. The defense were behind dummies and used sticks. It was one sided in favor of the attacks. Here's hoping it will be that way when we "go over the top" but it is fun and interesting and mighty instructive.

The trenches are made to conform in every detail except no concrete or steel is used. Over there they use that in their shelter holes which are supposed to be shell proof.

We have drawn all our equipment now, unfortunately for we have to wear heavy marching order for drills now. It is not terribly tiring tho, but when we are actually on the

---

20 K.S.A.C. stands for Kansas State Agricultural College and it is now Kansas State University.

march it will be about twenty pounds heavier, for we only roll a blanket up empty now.

It serves the purpose but when on the march we will have to have clothes, shoes, toilet articles, etc.

I was lucky enough to draw a young spade to carry, too — four to a squad.

Right now I am a signalman, whether I stick depends on how good I am and how many are needed. Rather like it and get out of drill in the afternoon.

We are due to leave here next Wednesday. Nothing official of course because we don't get those things, officially till the night before. But it is quite likely true for the officers have been telling us for weeks that we were going shortly.

Will probably get paid Monday and draw clothes and lay around Tuesday getting ready, and shove off Wednesday.

Write me here tho and I'll let you know new address as soon as I know.

Lots of love,
TOM

Letter to Mother, September 30, 1917

Quantico, Va.

Dear Mother:

I got a letter day before yesterday, written to me at Paris Island. Took it a long time to get around, but it finally did. I must have another one or two yet somewhere between here and there according to those since.

Were out to the trenches today and took some pictures, also took some in camp here. Will send some when they are finished; hope they are good.

Our new chaplain is here now, the one who will go with the 6th to France or wherever we go. The latest dope now is that we are to leave next Sunday—one week from today, so you see it's not certain, and maybe a month before we actually sail. The second and third battalions will leave here together. We also heard that the first was not in France but still up at N.Y. waiting for us and we'll all go together.

Didn't get any mail so far today but will at seven o'clock tonight I guess. Expect I'll get a letter from you then.

The third battalion was out on a hike one day last week of about ten miles. I expect we'll get ours this week. Will not come hard now tho for we do more than that, I imagine every day at drill; and now of course drill is with full equipment, that is heavy marching order.

The artillery had a field day the other day. I didn't get to see any of it except the end—the push ball contest. Was on police duty. The push ball looked like good sport—the first time I ever saw a game of it. Pretty rough as carried on by the "Marines" tho as they get "hard" right now over most anything.

Well must close this now.

Lots of love to everybody,
TOM

Letter to Ted, October 4, 1917

Quantico, Va.

Dear Ted:

Guess you will be getting pretty old by the time this reaches you.[21] Have you started shaving yet?

I got Vee's letter and also Viv's the other day. You tell them I will answer soon.

---

21 Ted's birthday is October 6.

How is school coming? And how many fights have you had? How is your girl or rather your girls?

We had a big regimental parade this morning, took every inch of space we could find on the parade grounds.

We have heard lots of things today. Some say we are going Sunday, others say we will be here for a month yet and of course necessarily we are not told much about it.

I am sending you a shell like we shoot in our guns, only this one is decorated a little. Pull the bullet out and use the "powder."

Must close this now.

Lots of love,
TOM.

Letter to Vee, October 8, 1917

Quantico, Va.

Dear Vee:

I got your letter today. Am about all in tonight. We hiked all day today and yesterday. Of course we hiked all over Washington streets and parks and all.

We left here about one o'clock Saturday and when we got to D.C. went over to the Capitol and simply stumbled into the closing session of Congress. We didn't even know they would be in session. Our uniforms got us in and we spent about a half hour in the Senate Chamber and heard a lot of hot air from a Senator Call, I believe from N. Mexico in a very pointed if not personal harangue of Senator La Follette. I wish we had gotten there sooner and heard La Follette. He gave a very hot one from what the papers say. He had the floor for a few minutes several times while we were in there.

You sure have to admire him no matter what you think of his convictions. He surely is a finished man and a

splendid talker. Sure showed up every one else who was
on the floor during our short stay.

There were not many there. About 30. Poor old Call,
every one butted in on his speech because there was a lot
of little things that had to be finished up. Nobody paid
any attention to his spiel except reporters and spectators.
A fine line about the wealth of our grand old country and
paying for the war out of natural resources. Finally after
many interruptions which would have ruined a good
speech, he managed to get in a grand eloquent finish and
they immediately adjourned.

We were present when they made Pershing and Bliss
Generals. Other measures were voting salaries to dead
officers' wives and vote of thanks to president of senate
and president pro tem.

We were so situated in the gallery that we couldn't see
the chair. There was an awful crowd, so we didn't get to
see Marshal.

After they adjourned we looked it all over, also
the House Chambers and the Supreme Court parlor.
Everything governmental is surely marvelous. Beautiful
marble everywhere, furniture all mahogany.

Wilson was there but we didn't see him either. We
didn't go in either the Senate or House office buildings,
which are about two blocks away on either side, parking
in between; they are sure splendid buildings.

The most marvelous thing there is the Congressional
Library. It is a couple of blocks in front of the Capitol,
parking in between of course. The building itself from
the outside is beautiful of course, but inside is simply
indescribable. It cost six and a half million dollars. Simply
a wealth of mosaics, friezes, inlays and marble. The ceiling
in the congressional reading room is satin with paintings
in solid gold. Mosaics which cost thousands of dollars and
made of gold. They have guards all over. I had to check

my kodak. The building itself is a rare treat simply to go thru, and look at and then the books and manuscripts, some rare originals, all under cover of course, some of Washington's orderly's books etc., orders to Braddock and the like. Early English stuff.

If a person had a year say to go thru it, he could get something out of it, and we trying to go thru in a few hours, you can see how we had to skim. Then the paintings and etchings and Chinese and Japanese books written on palm leaves, etc. A reproduction of the Rubayait smaller than the butt end of this pen. The building is shaped like this—

The front part has all these exhibits, the squares there are open parks and around on those wings are the books, three stories high and two basements. The circle represents the main reading room and over this is the dome made of solid gold. The desks in it are arranged in a great circle about the desk and you go sit down and they bring the book you want right to you. You can't get in to the alcoves since the war, so there was one whole wing that we couldn't go thru, but we saw too much as it was to really appreciate any of it.

Then the museum, another new building in the richest of marble, everything marble and grand. Have simply everything there. Indian relics and dress, dishes and weapons, rugs and blankets that would make Po simply bawl. Oh, if we could only have had time to really look at a few things. Geological formations, some meteoroids from Kansas, other places too. Reproductions in miniature of palaces in Yucatan which are marvelous. Mummies, skeletons of extinct animals and prehistoric ones. One sea animal 78 feet long. Mounted specimens of every kind, bird, beast, and bug I guess, under the sun, including those presented by the Roosevelt East African Expedition. Pianos and organs from the year one. Art exhibits, a model

of the first heavier air machine which was first in flight at
Quantico, Va.

Then the Treasury Building, we didn't go in but it is a
beautiful building and you would recognize it for what
it is the moment you lay eyes on it. Near it the White
House in grand grounds, but couldn't get a very close view,
and no one is allowed in the grounds. Covers about four
blocks.

The old Riggs National Bank is opposite the Treas.
Building. They have a fine building more on the lines of
the government structures than the other banks. They had
the big fuss with the Controller of the Currency a couple
of years ago.

About ten minutes walk back from the White House
is the Washington Monument. We went up. Sure get a
grand view. Is many times the highest thing in the vicinity.
Every state has a stone and every Masonic Grand Lodge
also, I guess every lodge and society in the country. I never
realized before, the thing was made of marble. Not fine
polished slabs as in the buildings but a coarser marble in
enormous blocks.

To the west of it is the Lincoln Memorial in the process
of construction which will be a beautiful building.

We only hated that we didn't have time to go out to
Arlington Cemetery and Fort Myer, etc. but couldn't do
everything.

Altogether had a fine time, got a bed, which was rather
fortunate when Congress is in session and everyone from
three military camps come in, for it was our first liberty
since pay, and Camp Mead the conscript camp, fort Myer,
the officers engineers and aviation, as well as Marines.

Wore ourselves out recognizing army officers on the fly.
The Marines are getting the devil for not saluting them
and we never had a chance to see an army officer before,
so we have to watch, for in the army a buck private can

wear as good clothes as an officer. No such luck in the old Jireens.

Also they have a splendid union depot. We got home about nine o'clock and were ready for bed. I took some pictures; will send them later.

Tonight it is raining and I'm going to turn in right away. Stan had a telegram from V.O. W. Says he has "resigned" from officers camp and is trying to get with us. I'm afraid he can't do it tho, I sure do wish he could, he would be a good bunkie. No more news as to our departure.

Lots of love,
TOM

Letter to Doc, October 9, 1917

Quantico, Va.

Dear Doc:

Got your letter a few days ago, and intended to answer before, but you know S.O.S. (such old ----).

Was up at Washington Saturday and Sunday. Didn't exactly paint the town red as it is dry to soldiers and supposed to be to civilians, but is practically wide open.

We went to the Gaity Saturday night to a good burlesque, nothing extra, same old leg show, tho they had a few new gags. Sure had good costumes, tho very little to them.

Laid in bed Sunday morning till nine o'clock for the first time since June. Really intended to go to church but could'nt find the right one so didn't.

Mainly took in the public buildings. Saw the game — world's series — on the electric diamond which showed every play and throw as it was made.

Washington is a little hard to get around in till you get used to it. Penn. Ave. runs thru and is the only street that does. The rest all run in to the Capitol. The main part of town is in northwest.

Yesterday had a long hike with bread and soup for dinner; everyone was about all in at night.

Today is rainy and damp and cold and everyone is freezing. Went out this AM but came in after an hour of bayonet work and have been getting signal practice in the bunk house since.

Heard today from our Lt. that the boat we go on will be a fast one — 23 knots — and will be convoyed, so that there is very little danger of U-boats for they are not very effective for a speedy boat. Most of the victims are freighters not making much over 16 knots.

We will not go before next week and maybe not then. Hope we get our winter field uniforms.

Have had to stop now. They have started class again. Now have a telescope sight on a rifle, but there is such a crowd you can't get near it yet.

Our platoon leader, the Lt. is a Tenn. college man and a big football player. He is a regular fellow. Is a Phi Gamma Delta, our chief rivals at C.C. They had some good men there all right and have all over I guess.

Stan gets his corporal strips in a few days. It may sound like sour grapes, but I don't care for the job as it is sure a rotten one. You get it from all sides and I'd rather be a buck private, I believe for all the $6.00. Of course there is some honor in it, but they break them about as fast as they make them, so if I get one I hope it will be after I've had a little real experience over there. Then I won't lead my eight men to a death trap. Some of the N.C.s don't know a thing and never will and of course some are really capable.

About two thirds of the company got on report today for carrying their ponchos out in their packs. Was the natural thing to do as it was wet and rainy, but we had orders last week not to carry them. I was lucky and didn't have mine.

Po's sweater sure comes in good these days. Wouldn't be so bad if it weren't wet, but suppose it wouldn't be cold then.

Think V.O. is too changeable to get in the service because once you are in you are in, and you've got to stick no matter what and they can do anything to you they want to in time of war.

Tell Vee not to worry about the pictures she sent to Paris Island. Didn't amount to much anyway. The reason we don't get it is because we didn't go with the main part of the company. They went to New Jersey. I expect I'll be broke when we hit N.Y.

Have quit our Patomic plunges.

Push ball is a big ball, shape of a basket ball but six feet in diameter and they push it on a field the size of a football field. In case of a deadlock it usually goes up in the air and sometimes they keep it in the air quite a ways.

Must close.

Lots of love,
TOM.

Letter to Dad, October 12, 1917

Quantico, Va.

Dear Dad:

Got your letter with Ted's and mama's. Much obliged for all the clippings. Ted is getting to be some penman, I think.

Think if the weather there is like here, you had better get the glass in the green house. It has been rainy here for the last three days, but we only missed one day and this afternoon. It is still drill time so I am beating the gov't time in writing this for I should be signaling.

Hope the florist turns out to be a good one.

You bet I'd rather catch a .30 cal. bullet than a bayonet any day. The ugly part about that is, the Dutch dum-dum them which is a court martial in civilized armies.

You had better be careful about publishing my letters. They probably need a good deal of editing, for half the time I don't suppose my sentences make sense.

This week we have been formed in sections—about 12 or 14 men each and drilled in skirmish work. Went out to the trenches yesterday and charged them with Brig. Gen. LeJeune as chief spectator. He has recently been put in charge of this post so I suppose Col. Catlin will go with the Sixth regiment. He was C.O. here.

We charged about 200 yards going forward in eight waves of skirmish line; the first had to jump in and clean up. We went thru barb wire entanglement and all.

This morning also we had some out on the parade ground. One bunch charged a pile of railway ties, and the captain and a few privates were behind them (which they didn't know) and they met them with a bunch of mud balls. The captain sure is a good sport as are all the Lts. One is "hard"—a man up from the ranks—he is a constant reminder of our dear Paris Island.

This PM it rained so we didn't go out. Went up to draw clothes and they got a pair of leggings. Haven't any of my winter field yet, tho quite a few have gotten them.

We expected the guard tonight but fortunate for us it was transferred to the 8th regiment. Still have no more news of leaving. But officers still insist before the first of the month. Matter of fact I don't think they know any more than any of us.

Am looking for some pictures tonight and will send some if I get them.

Had a letter from granny today. Glad she is still getting along nicely. Also had one from Lois; she seems to be liking it better than at first.

We are having it fine here, only still a scarcity of water. Have to get up half an hour before reveille nearly to get any to wash your face. Can't wash clothes and are not supposed to send them to the laundry tho there are no orders against it and over half the company do.

Well must close this,

Lots of love,
TOM.

Have been up town and back and didn't fall down once. Guess you know what Virginia mud is like tho.

We got our "dog license" yesterday. Has name, branch of service and date of enlistment.

Yours,
TOM.

Letter to Helen, October 18, 1917

Quantico, Va.

Dear Helen:

Got your letter today and will answer right away as I have an easy graft today, for once. Got put on police duty, which is soft here. Worked this AM till about ten o'clock and then washed some clothes for myself. This PM I made one trip down to the regimental quartermasters which took all of ten minutes and no more work in sight for the day.

I am slated for some clothes today, they have gotten some more in, seem to have an awful time outfitting them. Each company has to almost fight to get anything.

We didn't get away as expected; there were a couple of companies that did leave tho. We really know nothing about when we go and it is rumored that we will be the last to leave, that is the last of the sixth.

The eighth is forming at this post now. About 900 men came in from Mare Island via Panama last week. Our mess sergeant said today we'd probably go about the 25th but I doubt if he knows any more than the rest of us.

We have been working pretty extensively in skirmish and field drill in section units instead of squad. The section is anywhere from 12 to 24 men and are in charge of a gunnery sergeant, four sections to a platoon. One section Bombs, two sections riflemen, and one section machine gunners. I am in the bombies. They use the hand grenades and will be equipped with .45 colts as well as rifles, we are practically armed to the teeth. But they are the first to go over so need to be.

We went out to the range here one PM this week and shot two ranges two and three hundred yards and shot in all positions, merely for practice, it won't affect our qualifications. I shot a little below sharpshooter still, but we shot in standing position which is very unsteady and the sling is almost valueless. I made only 16 out of a possible 25.

We have stoves in the bunk houses now so I guess we won't freeze to death. It is cloudy and damp today but no rain so far. Is a little unpleasant so I'm just as glad I didn't have to go out.

Each platoon is getting up a football team. Our team is to play the first Friday, only for practice. The first platoon are the big guys. The fourth the little ones. I'm going to try to hold down a guard.

I'm sure glad Viv is going to school. He'd sure be foolish to pass it up, a good chance and there's no time like the present. Sure he'll get along fine, there's a lot in getting a start tho. I hope he'll get started off right and I guess there'll not be much danger of homesickness, with you there and he's been away from home a good bit anyway.

There is sure a pretty country around here and suppose Eastern Kansas is more like it here. It's all woods and hills except small patches. The trees are surely pretty too, it's a treat go get to go out to them.

The trenches and the range are both about a mile from camp thru the woods and I appreciate the hike every time we take it, tho the road is a fright.

I have taken seven shots for typhoid and not one made me sick, tho they all made the arm sore for a couple of days of course. It affects different people in different ways but we had only a few that it made sick. It is really a good thing I believe, tho it's kind of like having a tooth pulled, you keep putting it off, only of course we didn't. Ordinarily they stick you $25 or $30 for it, don't they?

Think you are doing fine on the Y.W. The "Y" here has entertainments every night, only the building is too small. Once a week they have vaudeville or singers from outside, rest of the time movies.

I would like to see Camp Funston. It must be a large camp. I sure wish you could see our Marines drill here tho. They are getting mighty good and it really is a sight to see a large body of soldiers drill together and never a bobble. The chief trouble is in hearing commands in a regimental drill. The commander stands in front and we are third company in senior battalion and I in the last platoon, so usually are about a hundred yards away, and every man has to hear to keep it from being ragged.

Really we are comfortable here and well fixed except for getting up at 5:30. You know how I like that and four months of it hasn't made me like it any more. Will four years, I wonder?

Our chow is fine almost as good as the menus you see published in papers about what the soldiers eat at the training camps. Most any I ever saw were stretched a good deal or else the army and navy eat much better than the Marines, and they all have the same allowance. We don't have butter but about once or twice a week. We do have good meat here which we never did on the island. Also our cook knows his business.

They are concreting all the streets in camp and when they get an adequate water supply, it will be almost ideal. I shouldn't mind staying here all winter. It will be better than tents or billets in France, but just the same they can't make us sore to jerk us out right soon.

The fifth regiment of Marines now in France never got to the trenches, but was split up and are in service as provost guards. We may get the same thing when we do get there.

Lots of love,
TOM.

Letter to Mama, October 19, 1917

Quantico, Va.

Dear Mama:

I got your letter with Ted's clippings yesterday. Tell him much obliged. Also got Vera's today.

We have a fire in our stove tonight as it is raining again. We got in before it started but went out to play football so of course it started in and has been at it ever since. Otherwise it has been warm this week here.

We had a funeral here today. Didn't get to see but the start of the parade as they sent us in to clear the parade ground for the procession. A private in one of the artillery companies. A tree fell on him and crushed him when they were cutting it. The hearse was an army truck but the coffin was wrapped in the Stars and Stripes and the flag was at half mast.

Have not been working very hard of late and have something different nearly every day. This PM we had some new open order formation for attack.

If we are still here in two weeks from now I think I'll go up to Washington again. At the present I'm financially embarrassed.

Glad you got a car turned. The houses if good ones ought to bring a pretty good price.

Vee sure seems to be flying around and I guess had some time at her Eastern Star "do." We have about a dozen masons in the company that I know of.

I didn't suppose Po would stick at Spearville very long.

The trench pictures weren't very good. The sacks are sand bags, very effective in stopping a german bullet. The peep holes are fixed like this. At X are the peep holes which gives each rifle a range of nearly 90 on the horizontal, so they must all be occupied or the enemy will flank you because you can only cover a certain part of the front thru them. The machine guns are stationed at the flank of each platoon. Thus:

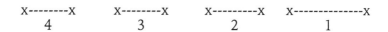

```
X--------X      X--------X      X---------X    X--------------X
    4               3               2                1
```

X is the gun and the dash the platoon; then they cross fire in front of the platoon so you can see how much more thick they fly in front of the platoon. This forms quite a protection for the infantry and is almost a barrage fire (small). The barb wire is usually shattered by artillery fire now. We are issued two pairs of insulated nippers tho. I unfortunately drew a pair.

The Post sure has some good trench stories. Tells some of the tricks and schemes that have been used. One, a phosphorous post; the germans stuck up some stakes painted with phos. In no man's land and at night when a man scouting got in front of the post, he blotted it out of course and they potted him. An old Canadian trapper went out to figure out why they got so many men and noticed the posts and went out the next night with a board, and then fired on the flash as the germans shot. They always shoot twice, he said to make sure, so he get his point of aim the first time and let go on them the second. He went all along the line that night and the germans quit using the phos. stake.

By the way I wish you'd send me that black jersey of mine. It is in my trunk I think and also the set of coat and trouser hangers in a leather cover there. They are kind of sporty to be using here, but have some clothes now and they will collapse when I want to pack up to move. I'll run the risk that we'll still be here. I'm figuring on another pay day here anyway, if not all winter.

If that roll collar can be taken off jersey easily, jerk it off, otherwise no matter. I can turn it under and in real cold weather it might be handy.

The ponchos are warm but unhandy. You put your head in the center and let it fall over you. The sides button up, making a big kimono sleeve. When in the field you put it down and lay your blanket on it. Keeps the damp from the ground out. We have drawn our dog tents too, now. Each man has a half tent and two bunk together. Each carries a collapsible pole about three feet high, also stakes.

Letter to Folks, October 24, 1917

Quantico, Va.

Dear Folks:

Well, "me say dam again." The third battalion left today and we had the pleasure of being honor guard. It would have all been very nice but it rained all AM so we were out for over an hour in the mud and slush. Still we shouldn't kick for we haven't had to drill today at all. Instead we wrote insurance, made allotments, and bought liberty bonds.

I am now worth $13,000 in black box, so don't know but what I'd better get submarined. Out of 265 officers and men in the company, we took out $2,620,000 of insurance. Wouldn't that be pickings for an insurance agent? Had one man on furlough, one who didn't take any, two who took $5,000, the rest all took $10,000, the limit. Costs me $6.50 month or $78 a year. This is the only insurance you get before you pay for it. Your Nov. insurance for instance comes out of Nov. pay on Dec. 1st.

You can continue to carry it for five years after the end of the war at same rate and can then convert it into 20-pay or anything, the terms to be determined later, but probably equally as liberal. In case of death the beneficiary gets $57.50 monthly for 20 years which will figure $13,800 in all. In case of disability I get that amount for life, if bedridden I get an extra $100 monthly.

In case of partial disability, we get paid on percentage basis according to injury. If you come out whole but within one year get a medical certificate of symptoms of disease contracted during the war you can at any time later in your life get compensation by presentation of certificate, if you are disabled thru these said causes or symptoms, this separate from insurance.

Yesterday the company was on the range. We fired 75 rounds a piece and came in pretty well tired out at night. We had dinner out there from our field kitchen. I shot sharpshooter on all the way thru except the last range. It rained all PM, just a drizzle not enough to stop us but enough to make it cold and mean, also bad light. On our 15 trial shots on three ranges, I made 66 out of a possible 75—expert. Then on the other 60, I made 223 out of 300. The last range, the hardest, 500 rapid fire—it was dark as usual—the last range. I only made 26 but a score above 30 was rare and more than a few didn't make a thing. No wind here and it's fine shooting only after that many shots your shoulder begins to get a little sore, especially if you let a couple slip out of place a little. If it slips more than a little, you get a crack on the nose or eye from the cocking piece or locking lug.

The company had eight machine guns on the range. They simply eat up ammunition. Each load is 47 shots and is fixed by simply pulling the trigger and holding it; if released it stops firing. They are capable of 600 per minute, but it is never done because the ammunition is never plentiful enough and it has to be reset after each 47. Of course, if they had it on a heavy tripod that would be done away with, but lastly the cooling system is not adequate for that, five or ten minutes of firing at that rate would eat up the barrel. They are air-cooled. They are taken down simply by a shell that is the only tool necessary. Every pointer must be able to take down and assemble one blindfold so that he can do it at night when no lights are allowed in France.

Well we still have no more idea than before of when we will go. Our major is senior and had choice of going this time or next. Well he elected to wait, so here we are. We expect another pay day here anyway, the 25th.

Had fire call last night at just twelve o'clock; the officers club burned down. They have a new one all built, so now suppose they will go right in; the old building was a frame shack and burned to the ground.

Only half our company was ordered out, the rest of us had the pleasure of "standing by" in the company street, which was no fun at all; if you have to get up for a fire you want to get to it. Got to bed about one, again, but busted up the night's sleep quite effectually.

This AM the artillery are firing down the river so we are drilling under cover of them. A couple of nights ago they were firing down from Indian Head, the heavy coast guns, you could see the flash and almost a minute after, you could hear the thunder of the explosion. Needless to say all boat traffic is suspended when they are firing. Gen. Lejeune was out watching hits.

Well must close this for now.

Lots of love,
TOM.

Letter to Helen, October 29, 1917

Quantico, Va.

Dear Helen:

I got your letter several days ago and had guard yesterday so didn't get it answered as I expected to. We mounted guard at four forty five and I happened to be on the third relief, the hard one by the way and didn't get off till seven o'clock Sunday night. We had the late relief and the new company is always late. We had a good night except the first relief got rained on good and proper. It sure poured for a half hour and we were sure glad we were on the third then. I had a good post. Inside the base hospital guarding two prisoners. Had a nice fire and

could sit down and everything, only had the satisfaction
of knowing I'd get a "general court" if they got away from
me. They both were "generals" waiting for their hearing
tho they were both old timers and expected to get off. The
old men can get by lots of things.

We had movies taken of us last Friday; we did the
manual and a few live movements, other companies did
bomb throwing, trench work, etc. Also we have been
having some special English training which is unwritten
and so I can't tell you anything about it. Our platoon
walked away with all honors on doing it tho.

We had a fire call one day last week and had to get out
at twelve o'clock and then didn't get to go to the fire. Only
half the Co. did.

You sure seem to be living a fast life there. Gee, but a
fellow's college days look good when you're "looking back"
on them, tho you may not appreciate them so much when
you're there. Am sure tickled for your Omicron Nu. Did
your Washburn Sorority make its national?

We have not had any cold weather here to speak of.
Have had lots of rain tho, making it plenty sloppy.

Stopped here and went to chow. It's raining again now.

The third battalion left last week and are aboard
transport now. Some of the boys here had censor cards
from them. We expected to go before them but we still
stick here, and know no more than before.

We practiced a little today on some fancy
manual — "silent Manual." Go thru 50 counts at one
command. Is pretty hard to get 250 men to do that many
without a single bull. I was in front and couldn't see but
we did it well enough to make the captain look tickled so
guess it was pretty good.

Say, I have a little Masonic pin at home you have a right
to wear if you like. Vee, belongs to the Eastern Star so she

doesn't need it. It might help you traveling around. My lodge is Spearville 388.

Sure got a deluge of eats this week. Got a package from Vee, and one from Aunt Minnie Saturday, and today got a couple from Lois. Sure have had lot of friends too, believe me.

Guess we'll get a pay day this week. Are so close to Washington that we get paid about the first. Suppose over in France we'll be about a month late.

See the Sammies are now in the first line trenches in France. Italians seem to be losing in their drive again. Well must close this.

Lots of love,
TOM

Letter to Bob, November 5, 1917

Dear Bob:

I'm sending you a little stone. They pick these up out in the hills of Virginia.

This one is finished off and polished but they are found in cross shapes like this. They are called fairy stones.

I have written to mama so I can't write much now.

Tell somebody to beat you on the back for me.[22]

Much love and many kisses,
TOM.

---

22 Bob's birthday was November 6.

Letter to Mama, November 5, 1917

Quantico, Va.

Dear Mama:

Got your two letters and also one from Vee since I last
wrote. Glad you finally got the glass for the green house.
If it is like here you would need it all right. I noticed a
fourteen degrees for Dodge one day, tho and that beats us
I guess. Gets cold as the deuce at night here but in the day
time when the sun comes out, we soon get hot at drill of
any kind, so hardly know how to dress.

Dad will surely have to get someone to help him in the
greenhouse, it will be more than you can do.

Aunt Minnie wrote me they had eight inches of snow up
there. We haven't had any yet but they say at Camp Taylor
in Kentucky the boys are suffering from the cold; they
haven't complete outfits yet.

I wouldn't send anything to France for I doubt if we
even make it by that time now and besides they might
hold it up at New York on account t of us not being over
there, for they don't want an ounce of shipping that isn't
almost a necessity. I'd take the chance anyway of not
sending it. According to latest reports now we're to spend
Thanksgiving here and if we do that we may be here yet
another month.

Yes, the 6th Reg. has all gone but the 2nd battalion and
the first battalion is assuredly in France; the other, I know
not. The Italians seem to have lost all they had gained. If
they can hold now tho it will still be all right.

Stan and I were up at Washington Saturday and
Sunday. Saw a peach of a show at the Belasco. I'll send
you a program, but it will mean little, I guess. Went
to the Congregational Church—could not find the
Presbyterian—and had looked it up too. Got a bid out to

dinner and of course took it. A little chap about Ted's age wanted a soldier for dinner and so we got a real feed.

The lady lives over in Georgetown, which is what they call the underground city on account of the exclusiveness of the society, etc. Georgetown was a city before Washington was laid out.

This Mrs. Lewis has lived here almost all her life. Mr. Lewis is a lawyer. She certainly did show us a good time. Is a true southerner and the whole place was ours. She said now come back and I'll not get anything extra ever for you, but you are welcome to what we have; and asked us out for the night next time — have a big house. Mrs. Lewis is a cousin of Col. Longstreet now commanding Camp Jackson in S. C. He is a descendant of Gen. Longstreet of civil war fame.

Well first when we left the church we got into the Buick and drove out thru the park and the drive along the river. It is lined with cherry trees from Japan on one side and willows on the river side. Then home to dinner of chicken, licking mashed spuds, cold slaw, salsify, pickled peaches, gravy, peaches and cream and cake. Mrs. L. apologized for the cake. A "store boughten one" said she couldn't get any sugar in Washington. Is it that bad out there? Meals are high here but I didn't realize it was anything like that.

They have a boy 10 years old, one 14, and a girl, but unfortunately at boarding school and so not at home.

After dinner went out 16th St., millionaire row. Lots of interesting and historic places that we couldn't ever have known but for someone like her. She enjoyed showing it all. Then we went out thru the Zoo and back up around, and across the river to Fort Meyer, went all thru it, and then thru the Arlington Cemetery. It is certainly wonderful as is the Lee Mansion in the center of it. The Confederate monument is just new and is a splendid piece of work. Admiral Dewey's Tomb is splendid. Is really Gen.

Miles Tomb. Dewey is resting there till the Gen. Sees fit to use it himself. They haven't built Dewey's own yet. Miles tho is on a knoll and is almost the most desirable location in the place—a splendid view of the city and everything.

Well by now it was about five and we drove back to the city and said goodbye.

There are lots of French and English officers and M.C.O.S. out at Fort Meyer training the officers there. Also saw Italian officers and a Scotch "lady of hell." That's what the Huns call them. I thot perhaps I'd get to see Bob Hood, but didn't run on to his battery and didn't like to take too much time to hunt him up. If I'd been alone, it would have been different.

Got a close up at the wireless towers at Arlington. They are second only to Eiffel Tower as the highest wireless towers in the world.

Today we went on a hike and had some skirmish work over the hills.

Our menu for today was—breakfast: beans and coffee. Dinner: Marine stew and cocoa. Supper: roast beef and succotash. Bread is served with all meals. Some come down from yesterday.

Well must close this now.

Lots of love,
TOM.

Letter to Folks, November 18, 1917

Quantico, Va.,

Dear Folks:

The Marine is sure an ingenious animal. This morning two or three kids in our platoon made a violin out of the usual cigar box and deuce of it is, one of them can play it. They got it tuned up and he drags some real music out of it.

We are on guard again today. It makes me no difference particularly for I'm not on and when we're on on Sunday the rest don't have to work like they would otherwise. Most likely we'll draw it Thanksgiving day too. It comes every ten days, and we have had it three Sundays out of four times on guard the last six weeks. The whole company loses liberty is what makes everybody crab. Part of them went up to D. C. for a provo guard, too.

Had the privilege of hearing the Head of the Religious Dept. of the International Y.M.C.A. speak this AM. He is certainly a splendid Talker, and knows how to appeal to his men. Has been all over the front and before the war was in every country in Europe except one, engaged in this work. Has traveled extensively in four continents and it has made a remarkable man of him.

I sent you a "Marine Leatherneck" yesterday. It is the post paper and that the first edition. Has a little pretty good stuff in it. Some one has discovered why the Marine is always first and so eager to fight: "When we die we know we're bound for heaven, for we've done our hitch in hell."

Three battalions came over from Philly the other day, mostly artillery, so at present the infantry here are almost a negligible quantity. Two battalions of infantry, one of machine guns, and three or four thousand artillery men on our side of the creek. The artillery camp is too small to hold all of the original companies. Also an officers training school. They are sure fixing up the range here fine. Have two ranges of 24 targets each, the butts together, but the firing lines split on account of a hollow. The one now, they are making 800, 1000, and 1200 yard ranges are for expert riflemen course. Use a 28-in. bulls eye on these ranges. The artillery range is about completed now too, so they don't have to use the Potomac. Indian Head keeps booming away at us about every other night. It is just like a thunder storm. A flash away up there and then later on a rumble that makes the ground shake.

They are building a big new "Y" and plan to have entertainments and dances next month Also they are going to have Masonic club rooms up town pretty soon, so this may not be such a bad place to winter after all.

If we could only have a little condensed water for use at any time.

I guess you spotted me all right in the picture. Stanley is in the front row, I believe on the extreme left of the picture. Had a letter from our old friend in D. C. asking us up for Thanksgiving. Afraid tho we can't go.

Sure glad granny is getting along so well. I had a letter not long ago from her and it was written real well, a lot better than the one just before. Too bad you couldn't stay longer.

Hope the florist likes it there and you can make a deal of some kind.

Tell Vee I had an invite to a swell dance in D. C. for last night. Some Vassar college girls among those present. Our company draws the guard right away so I can't go. Anyway the kid who invited lost all his jack in a crap game so he didn't go either.

Floyd Bleger with the first battalion of the 6th was in England and is now probably in France. As I got the news rather indirectly. He has never written any of his pals here, including his bunkie from Hutchinson. that he shipped in the service with.

There is going to be a big blowout for Masons in uniform in D. C. next Saturday. I'm going to bust something to get there. A corporal who in N.G. owes me $3.00. I'll have to bean him and pawn his clothes I guess. It is a consolidation of all Wash. Masons in their first welcome to the khaki hosts. There sure is a mob of army camps right near Washington.

The sox Aunt Maude sent were sure swell and will be great when we get our trench boots. Weather is still too warm here for them. Had a couple of windy, cloudy days that nearly froze you stiff last week but today is lovely again.

Lots of love,
TOM.

Letter to Dad, November 20, 1917

Quantico, Va.,

Dear Dad:

Got your letter and Vera's and Bob's and Ted's and sure enjoyed them all. Had a letter from Nina today, also one from granny and Em.[23]

It was so crowded here tonight that I waited about fifteen minutes before I could get a place to sit down to write. I could write at the bunk house only we don't rate but about half enough lights and my bunk happens to be a dark one and don't like to bother some one else. They expect to get into the new "Y" next month.

I was issued a "gat" today. Just a little more to carry, keep clean, and prepare for inspection. Maybe will appreciate having one when we go over the top tho. (Colt automatic .45 model 1911, U.S.A.).

They are sure getting stiff with us. Were out today for a killing and they sure got them. Got no dirty guns in our platoon but were putting them up for office hours if you even turned your head at attention or moved a muscle. Of course you expect to get called on that but it's pretty stiff giving a fellow office hours for it. Two or three went up and didn't know what for and one fellow dropped a "stack"

---

23 Nina Irwin is referenced, Tom's cousin.

which is an unpardonable sin and didn't get a thing, so
you see it's not what you do or don't do you get credit for;
it's simply what you can get by with, and some of them
sure get by with murder. The guys they caught got a lot
of extra police work in preparation for a big inspection
tomorrow by Adj. Gen., I guess.

Yes the Italians lost a lot but no one can lay it at their
door. They knew all along what they were doing and
knew what the Germans were doing and if England and
France and even America had listened to her two months
ago, they would have been able to hold the line. The
Germans drove them back simply by great preponderance
of numbers. Never in this war has a German army or
detachment of equal size won a victory or held its ground
and it never will. Germany's location and splendid railway
facilities make it possible to shift her fronts with such
rapidity to handle twice the number of foe at bay. She
massed on Serbia and again against Russia and tried the
same old gag on Italy; all these after failing in the first
great one against France.

Every one talks about the internal condition of
Germany and it must be terrible but it is sure not
showing up much on the outside. She seems to be able
to put out grub and cannon for her army. The Italian
front is the one to win the war on. Too bad Uncle Sam
can't send troops there. Maybe she can relieve enough
French men to go turn the trick.

Financially Italy was the worst off before the war began
and even with the Allies backing is not very well fixed.

I really haven't been counting on Christmas at home
much as I should like to, for several reasons. First, our Lt.
couldn't get a furlough for Thanksgiving, so I imagine a
private would have a fat chance. Of course Xmas might
be different. Would depend on whether the C.O.'s wife

made the coffee to suit him that morning or not, largely, I suspect.

Another thing, it will take me about a year as it is to pay my debts on the princely salary of a private ($15/mo), so I guess I'll eat Xmas dinner with the 96th whether it be Quantico, Philly or France.

Yes, I have met Paul Russell. Don't know much about him; doesn't run with the "Elite" at least, in D. C. Either he or his brother used to go to Emporia. I met a kid on the Island who knew him, also knew the Weidower brothers. Heard thru Ward that Ed W. was going to join the colors when he got out of debt.[24] The quartermaster Dept. is apt to be a meaner job than plain soldiering, tho it's pretty soft for an old timer and of course some new men get it that way, too. More so in the army than in the Corps, for it is expanded, more and more places to fill.

Tell Vee, Nina said they had a blowout for one of the boys leaving there and had Fink's orchestra from C.S. and everything. Did I tell you or did you already know that Burgess had bought a hardware store there?

Say, Vee, wish you'd send me another of those pictures of me in khaki uniform — those last ones if you have gotten the films yet, you know which one I mean. I was sore after I ordered that company picture for a day or two later a photographer from W. took one that was a lot better, but I didn't want two and couldn't renege on this one.

Have never seen any mistletoe here, tho there is quite a lot of holly.

There was a big bunch came in this AM from P.I. Guess they go into the artillery companies, they are all incomplete, all the Philly companies.

---

24 Ed Weidower is referenced here. The Weidower's were friends of the Stewarts in Spearville.

See the Mines beat C.C. a couple of weeks ago. Didn't
see last week's results in Kansas or Colo. Half the time
the Washington paper doesn't print them. When it's not
there I always know C.C. wins. With the same reasoning I
suppose K.U. loses. Glad to see them beat old Okla. They
needed to. Our company team is practicing regularly now;
they plan to have three teams and keep using fresh men.
The artillery now has the jump on them all.

We are having close order this week, same old "squads
east" again. Had a parade today with the aid of the
artillery band.

Had better close this now.

Lots of love,
TOM.

Letter to Folks, November 25, 1917

Washington, D. C.

Dear Folks:

Made Washington again this week but am poor as a
church mouse now till pay day. Hear we are to have quite
a liberty for Thanksgiving: Wed. night till Monday reveille.

Stanley had quite an interesting letter from his sister
yesterday. Says the Wards are moving to Pueblo to take
a job there, quite an advance as they think. V. O. takes
Merle's job at Spearville but not his pay. May satisfy him
for awhile now tho Stanley still thinks he will go to war.
I do not think he will. What he can get into doesn't suit
him so it seems. He might of course. I imagine he and
Tom and Doc will all be there for some time yet.

Troops are still piling into Quantico. I guess the old
camp will be full before long at this rate. A bunch came in
day before yesterday from San Diego. From what they say
they sure had a soldier's Paradise there. Only drilled one

hour a day and had liberty every day from noon chow call till the next morning. That would be almost too much of a good thing tho, I'm afraid. But of course they aren't going over so suppose don't need such intensive training. The sixth seems to be the last of the Marines to go over and at the present rate they are sure slow about getting there.

Didn't get to see the Marine football game. They beat Camp Mead 29 to 0 tho. Eddie Mahon is captain of the Marine team. Our darn train was two hours and a half late leaving Quantico and didn't get in here till almost five. I was sure sore and almost wished I'd gotten off and stayed at home.

Saw a good show last night and didn't get up this morning at "first call" by any means.

Washington sure is an artificial burg. No business like you see in any other place. Purely capital. Not even any big auti show windows or rooms or anything of that sort. As I guess Samuel Blythe says it's all underneath. You don't see a thing, but the ball is rolling just the same.

It turned real cold yesterday and last night. The breeze is still sharp today but it is nice and sunny outside. Hope the major sees fit to make the uniform conform to the day when we start out again. He has us out in khaki one day and overcoats the next, and like as not the hottest day we wear overcoats.

Well must close this now.

Lots of love,
TOM.

Letter to Mama, November 30, 1917

Quantico, Va.

Dear Mama:

Got your letter today also one a day or so ago and Vee's as well as the package you sent. It was swell and still is as it has not all been devoured yet. I spotted the pumpkin pie the first thing I guess. They were sure fine and sure made it taste like Thanksgiving at home. The olives didn't break and everything was lovely and appreciated ever so much.

We certainly had a feed today for once in the Marine Corps. I doubt if one half the people in the country fared half so well. The tables were literally covered till you couldn't see the board. About half the company was gone on liberty but they couldn't have had any better dinner or more of it. And we surely have a good cook. Makes it taste like home cooking, not Marine chow. Had turkey first of all. All you could eat of it, mashed potatoes and dressing, gravy, celery, cranberries, two kinds of pie and two of cake, ice cream, nuts, apples and oranges, and cigars; don't think I've omitted anything unless it is bread and butter and coffee.

Everybody ate till they couldn't hold any more and then took a pie plate and piled it full and took it out with them. Was comical to see some of them sneak past the captain, but he didn't care what they took. Have no supper tonight but nobody wants any.

Was real cold last night and the mud and slush froze solid but loosened up again today and this evening is trying to rain again. I hope it clears up before the week is out so we won't have to lay around the bunk house the whole liberty. I have some clothes to wash but they won't dry so no use to wash them. Say, if you think about it send me about six of those plain handkerchiefs in my trunk.

Think there is quite a gob of them. If not never mind. Don't send any initial ones or anything like that.

Had a nice letter from Gertrude Westmacott this week. Had a letter from Colo., too, saying that a lot of my C.C. friends were now in France. Our Major is a brother-in-law of the Major General commandant of the Corps so he can go any time he pleases and it seems he's in no hurry to go.

Was on guard Tuesday and Monday nights. The adjutant said we put on the best guard mount he'd seen. My post was taken off in the morning so about nine o'clock I had nothing to do but lay around from then on. Lay around the guard house and be sound asleep when they called for another sentinel. They gave us sandwiches and coffee at the guard house about twelve o'clock, which tasted pretty good.

I had a letter from Viv last week. Seemed to think he'd like it, tho rather strenuous at first. His pal may be up here from the island now. I heard there were some came up last night, and there were only ten companies left down there.

Hope it was nice there today, so you all could go up to Spearville. Was a good program at the church. Would have liked to have heard it.

We haven't signed the payroll yet, so will probably be late getting paid this month, as there won't be a chance now until Monday to sign it and that means about Wednesday at the best for pay.

Yesterday on account of the snow the night before, stuck in the bunk house and had "Rules and Regulations for the Governing of the Navy." Largely regarding desertion and overstay of leave in time of war.

Yes, pretty nice for Deac at Spearville now; too bad to lose Mr. and Mrs. W. Deac will miss Mrs. on the books no doubt.

When actually in the field few men pitch their dog tents unless it is raining or snowing. It's warmer to wrap up in them: put your poncho on the ground first.

Don't worry, nobody goes longer than about two days without a shave. We have a Lt. that would simply eat him up. If you can't get water that's your hard luck but you'd better have a shave when you fall out. They have taken to giving extra police duty for anything like that. In spite of all that tho our captain, our "old man" is a prince. He knows more about the stuff than all the Lts. but they are all nice fellows, but inexperienced. The captain sure has his fun tho. He'll jump on some one hard enough to scare him to death and then turn around so the kid can't see him, laughing. Ordinarily he talks very slowly and enunciates very clearly so when he bawls something at you, everybody tends to biz.

Everybody living in the New England states or anywhere around here as far west as Ohio went home over the four days. The ill-fated sixth tho still can't get furloughs, at least not by fair means. Everybody that has gotten one has received a telegram of every sick relative, and very few seemed to be worried much over their condition, but it usually got the furlough. I'm not saying that they were faked but some at least looked to be.

Well I must close this now. Hope you all had a dandy time up at Spearville today and I sure want to thank you for all the good things you sent me. About enough to make you all a good dinner there, I believe. I'll have Thanksgiving all week now.

Lots and lots of love to everybody,
TOM.

Letter to Mama, December 7, 1917

Quantico, Va.

Dear Mama,

Got your letter today with the pictures. Must have been a real pretty service. Sure two cute little kids. Glad you folks all got to go up to Spearville. Know how the kids would cut up. How is little Elizabeth? As fat as Katherine?

I feel quite dressed up tonight. Just got some new clothes issued tonight and am wearing my new blouse. Sure fits skin tight.

A battalion of machine gunners is shoving off tomorrow, but not a chance for the "home guards." They have shoved up our reveille another half hour tho—now six thirty.

There are some Canadian officers coming to give us the finishing touches in bayonet work and bombing and will also give physical exercises. So they say it will be all different now for awhile at least. Our Lt. said we were now in our fourth period of training and there were four more of about three weeks each. I'll sure be glad if ever we do get out of a "boot camp." You can't rely on what these Lts. tell you tho, for they seldom know much more about anything like that than a private.

I have a bid—Stan, too—to a swell affair at the Washington club next week, Sat. night, thru a friend in D. C. Her daughter is also to be home, so we're figuring on being there.

Now listen, I don't want you folks to get me a thing for Xmas. In fact I think I'm a lot better off than any of you. Besides you gave me the watch for Xmas and that's enough. I'll have more to eat than you so, you had better keep that stuff, and I have knitted stuff galore. There is only one thing I'd allow, that is a rubberset shaving brush, small size, and that is absolutely all.

And everybody is stung for anything from me for I'm broke—it's chronic—payday or not. I sent ten to the bank and paid my debts and I think have $3.00 left so I'm comparatively well to-do, as I'm getting quite used to being without a dime.

The Red Cross has provided two sweaters, helmet and wristlets for all the men in the company that haven't already gotten them. They are issued just like Gov't. clothes, only you don't have to sign for them.

Well must close this now. I'm enclosing the pictures. Is sure good and quite an original idea. Remember now about Xmas.

Lots of love,
TOM.

Letter to Vee, December 17, 1917

Quantico, Va.

Dear Vee:

Got your letters, dad's mama's and the clippings, also your draft. Much obliged. I have made out an allotment payable to you for $20.00. I don't know whether it will start this month or not; it should. When it comes, keep out yours and send the rest on to the bank for deposit. I was going to make it out to the bank, but to save arguments, I made it out to a relative and hope it won't make too much trouble. While I'm in the U.S.A. that will leave me only $5.30, but if I want any, I'll write before it comes to you. When we go over, it will be $8.30, which they say is loads in France.

The liberty Xmas will be four days, probably no more. The Capt. is trying to get furloughs for those who haven't had them, but ten days is the limit and the condition transportation is now in, it would take me six days to make the round trip, and it would hardly be worth attempting for anyone in my fix. So I'll probably eat my turkey in Quantico.

We were issued gas masks today, and this afternoon practiced adjusting them. Got so the average was about eight seconds from the "gas alert" position to complete adjustment. They reduce a man's efficiency about 75% they say. We tried running and after about 100 yards at a dog trot, we could hardly get our breath.

Last week we had beastly weather. Cold and snow most every day. Only stayed in one day tho. Went right thru the rest. They have us unsling equipment and take off overcoats and drill around in fancy steps and double time to keep warm. At the end of this period of training, we are supposed to be able to get out with identification tags only and enjoy this weather. According to Washington reports 12 above is the coldest, seemed colder to us tho.

Stan and I went to Washington as we intended Saturday. The daughter Susanne got home from boarding school about an hour after we got there, so we met them at the depot.

Drove out home and had dinner, which was some feed, by the way, and then as Mrs. Lewis was one of the hostesses we beat it down to the dance about eight thirty.

The Washington Club is the most exclusive large club in Washington, so we were told, and we surely met Washington society. An Arctic explorer and his daughter, neither of whom spoke English, a daughter of a Congressman, two million dollar babies who were sure prunes, regular Fiji islanders, some one of the old 'cats' drug in so we were told.

The richest people in Washington with their sables and mink, and aside from all these, about a half dozen of regular girls, with whom you could have a dandy good time. One, a Miss Calvo, of the Cuban Embassy, who was

as cute as she could be. She spoke English very correctly
with an accent and talked very slowly, and tried a lot
to see that we had a good time, tho she had no special
interest. They have been in Washington for a long time
and she of course is well acquainted. Also a Miss Jones
who was simply great. I don't know anything special about
her. Jane's never are noted, I suppose, but she sure was a
queen and you simply had to have a good time with her
around. And last but far from least Susanne. She is 19 and
just home from Stuart Hall, at Stanton, so that accounts
for all shortcomings which are mighty scarce. She is a live
wire for fair. Reminds me a little of Lucy Leidigh and looks
a little like Bob, only has lighter hair and blue eyes. After
we came home we had creamed oysters.

The oysters are oysters here too; I never ate any like
them any place. But I forgot about the men at the party.
Stan and I were among the five enlisted men. The others
were medical corps men from the American University
in the city. Only one Marine officer. About a dozen Army
officers from 2nd Lt. to Capt., mostly from the American
U., but several from the field service, and engineers. Also
about a half dozen Naval officers. A young son of Josephus
Daniels who is quite as soft pated as his father, if not
more so, supposing of course that be possible.

A popular music writer, Susanne's brother, a couple of
hicks not even in evening dress, with the million dollar
crowd and the rest not important. I had a part of a Paul
Jones dance with the Fiji baby, and she could neither dance
nor talk, so I decided not to take the million. But it would
have been a treat to have seen this one. Her hair was what
made us call her Fiji Islander; it was a show for fair.

The Club used to be those of the Russian Embassy and
are simply grand. Splendid parlors, and reception halls,
and a tea room, then two small dance rooms connecting,
the largest, little larger than the hall at Spearville, but

some floor! Oak and smooth as glass. Music good but only piano. Their orchestra went back on them and they had to take what they could get.

The L.'s had a house full. One of the boys came home with them and also another girl was staying there for the night, but we never saw her.

Got up at nine AM to breakfast. Had waffles with butter, syrup and gravy. Also fried rabbit which was mighty good.

We went to church with Susanne to a little Episcopal church which she says she has adopted. It is down in the factory district of Georgetown, and is supported by a few well to-do people, among them Mr. L., I inferred, but largely is a mission church in every other respect. Susanne has a class of little ragamuffins who simply adore her and were tickled to death to see her again.

Back home to dinner. Had chicken, spuds, macaroni, spinach, pickle, biscuits, coffee, ice cream and cake. After dinner we played around in the music room and a couple of girl friends came in.

The little boy was sick. He is about Ted's size, is eleven and is a lively youngster and hated it pretty badly to have to stay in bed.

We left on the early train, 6:45, which was only an hour and a half late and no reports on it, so all we could do was wait at the depot, as it might leave us and we didn't care for an 11:30 train which might be two hours late. Got in before taps, tho, at that.

Our new auditorium was opened Thursday in a splendid snow storm. The Marine band from Washington was down and was the chief attraction in spite of the Major Gen.Commandant and old Josephus himself, both of whom gave us a talk, of which we heard not a word, there being about 7000 gyrenes there and we in the rear.

Only 67 pieces of the band were present. There are 125 in all, but oh those 67!! I never heard anything like them.

Never a break. Could make it sound exactly like a pipe organ (immense) or burst out in a Dixie or Marseilles, that made your hair stand even; could certainly handle their instruments. Then about the music with ship bugles bust out with a call. They can play those calls, too. Must have made some of our musicians sick to listen to them.

In the evening they entertained us awhile and then a Washington company gave us singing, and a bunch of girls some dancing, all of which was mostly N.G. Then the band played for a dance. Taps were put off till ten thirty. About 12 or 15 girls and 7000 Marines. Poor Billy Sunday should have been there. It would have smashed one of his dramatic statements, that you bet you never see the men dancing together. I managed to get a dance with a dame after knocking down six Marines and hypnotizing a couple of 'gobs' and then got one, two dances off. We were ready to start and they played the 'Star Spangled Banner' and it was all off. The band gave us our "Semper Fidelis" and played it right. That is our marching song and is nearly always used in 'review.' They also played the Marine Hymn which is being published. I will send you one when they come out. One of the entertainers sang in French, the Marseilles and the band also played it. But it always takes Dixie to bring the house down. There are a lot of southern men in camp, which accounts for it in part, I suppose.

I don't think you could name ten states which haven't representatives in our company alone, and most all are like that. We have only a few Mare Island men, so we are shy on the far west, but the ninth is composed largely of Mare Islanders and old timers.

All the band men have 'hash marks' all up their sleeves. None less than two and some as many as six or eight. Each one represents four years in the corps. They can't get into the band on their first 'hitch.'

Well I must close this. I guess the folks will all be home before I can write, so I won't write, tho I have a letter from Lois, Helen, and Viv, this last week. Let them all read this.

Lots of love,
TOM.

P.S. That allotment should come monthly for 12 mo. on or near the first. May be delayed for awhile at first, on account of such a rush.

Had our mess hall all decorated in holly tonight and the orchestra played. It's our own orchestra. Have one guy that is a whiz on the cornet.

Wrote this at the bunk house on a stationery box, so doubt if you can read it.

Letter to Folks, December 22, 1917

Quantico, Va.

Dear Folks:

I'm sending a few facsimiles of one of the privates in the 96 Co. U.S.M.C. Do as you please with them. Give granny's one and Uncle Harry's one and distribute the rest as you like. The "life size" one were thrown in. I didn't buy them. I got a couple with hat on to show the emblem; that is the only way you can distinguish the branch of service, but I thot the other the better picture..

We have been having lectures from the Canadian Captain. I would like to send you a page from a notebook. It would be interesting but for a time will be a little more valuable to me.

He is quite an Englishman. Has been in the big show since '14, on all British fronts in France and just came over in Nov. so has the latest dope. Is a very interesting talker and has loads of experience.

One very interesting thing, he says they no longer use the telephone in the trenches, as Fritz has a device to catch the message at a distance of 1000 yards, and, as often, they are only a hundred or so apart, it would be pretty soft for him. He says we'll see what they use when we get there. Enough to say it is efficient.

Half the company got ten day furloughs. I didn't put in. Could get no traveling time and the condition traffic is now in, it would take me six days at best for the round trip, provided I made good connections. The names were drawn, as too many wanted to go, so most of those left are disappointed in not getting to go. The worst of it is we go on with schedule. Drill and guard except on Xmas day. Guard Monday next and New Year's day. Lucky tho we didn't get it Xmas, I suppose. I think I'll only have to stand one of them. More, too, we have no liberty in sight till the rest get back Jan. 1, so we're stuck in Quantico for the holidays.

They are planning an entertainment at the Lyceum Xmas Eve. A dance provided the men get the girls.

Well must close this now. Will you go up to S. for Xmas? Merry Xmas to everybody and lots and lots of love,

TOM.

Letter to Dorto, December 28, 1917

"WITH THE COLORS"
YMCA
Quantico, Va.

Dear Dorto,

I got the package last night and was sure tickled & believe me the cake is licking and the candy too mighty good & I sure do thank you & Lucy for it. Guess you are getting to be quite a domestic science artist.

I guess you will still be at home so I'll write this to L. & if you only get one week suppose they will forward it to you. I wrote home and guess you will read that letter & I haven't much news since.

Was up at machine gun school again to-day & qualified blindfolded. All O.K. That is to take down & assemble the Lewis gun in less than 18 minutes. I did it in 8' 15" that on second attempt & 10' 55" the first so they kicked me out; said I was too good. Never did it in less than 6' with my eyes open so you see you've got to have it in your mind. The record done by expert is 3' something but few of them get down to six blindfolded.

Our ser gave us a lecture on the Lewis gun this PM, why it is the most desirable & its advantages and disadvantages.

It warmed up again to-day & melted so we have slush again but it looks like snow to-night.

We had a general muster yesterday & told to be prepared for a 'call to arms' at any time. We will have 15 min. to fall out prepared for 3 days stay in the field.

Our 'Scotty' tells us he's getting to put in a show for us. Will get the artillery here to fire over us & show us how it breaks up wire entanglements & head cover. It will be the same as a barrage we'll have to follow over there only comparatively small.

He says we've a fairly good show of being sent right to the front when we do get there as we're getting what the rest are getting in France.

He has certainly told us a lot of interesting things & is going to 'show' us them as well before we're thru' I guess.

Must close this now. Be sure & tell Lucy how good the cake is & tell her many thanks & keep a whole load of thank yous for yourself.

Lots of love,
Tom

Letter to Helen and Viv, December 30, 1917

Quantico, Va.

Dear Helen and Viv:

Got the package of cake or candy, which? Anyway it's mighty good and I've been putting said sabre into play with great dexterity. I will bite tho, what do you call it?

Hope you folks are not having as cold weather there as we are, for fear it will take more coal than you can get, as I hear there is a shortage out there. It was 15 degrees below last night and we were thankful we didn't have to drill. I went back to civilian life and went without breakfast for a couple of hours more in the old bunk. Would have frozen stiff but for our many bunkies' blankets, who were on furlough and whose blankets were not.

Our Highlander is going to raise the devil for us I fear. Operations will start next week out at the trenches. He says we have nice warm barracks so we won't mind getting out in the cold and wet. You tell 'em "Scotty!" He has left his classic garb in Flanders. He is going to put on a "little show" for us. Have the artillery give us a barrage to steady our nerves and show the effect on the wire. Says the casualties are usually about 2% but he doesn't want any, because it would hold up the regiment for an investigation. Is going to make over our trenches to exactly like they appear in Flanders.

Had a letter from Tom Westmacott telling us of his engagement to Phyl. Said she was hanging on his neck as he was writing. Wonder what Mrs. W. will do. Betty is on her way I guess.

I had quite an unexpected Xmas present from the First National Bank in the way of a deposit slip stating "Bonus." Was quite tickled to say the least.

Wonder if the folks got the pictures all right. I haven't heard since they would get them. But all mail is badly delayed here.

I have to keep moving. Sit here at my bunk and write till I get cold and then go down by the stove where it soon gets too hot and have to move back again.

Must close this for it's nearly time for supper and I must eat at least two meals.

Many thank yous to both of you for the loaf candy or cake. My bunkies all vote for K.S.A.C.

Lots of love,
TOM.

Letter to Mama, January 3, 1918

Quantico, Va.

Dear Mama,

Your letter came last night, I had been expecting one from what Vee told me or didn't tell me about the trip to Spearville. You sure had a time of it. Seems like something always happens.

I haven't much news, wrote about all I know to Vee, last night. Has warmed up to-day quite a little bit and is nice and sun shining.

That furnace at home does burn quite a slug of coal. We may have used too good a coal but last winter it used to take about 2 ton for 3 weeks in the cold weather and the water is not right I know. I used to fight them for Mrs. P. and finally put it writing a request for a test of the meter as per city ordinance but couldn't get any one to take it. Each one wanted to lay it on someone else but they did give a flat rate then and Jimmy R. admitted all along that it must be wrong but of course he wasn't reading the meters and said he had to make out the bill for what they turned in. There might be a leak but I never could find it.

If they will shut the intake valve in the cellar off a little it will stop the constant leak in the tank in the bath room for the cut off in it is not strong enough for the pressure. That is the way I fixed it.

Must have been an interesting club meeting in Spearville.

Mrs. Lewis' address is 1669 Thirty First st., Washington D.C. She certainly is good to us—treats us like she'd known us always and everything on the place is ours when we're there. Has a boy Ted's size that is quite a lad, sure interested in everything military and has quite a fund of information too. Must close now.

Love,
Tom

Letter to Helen, January 14, 1918

Quantico, Va.

Dear Helen:

Have been leading the life lately, on duty and off, so haven't had a chance to write, in reply to your letter, sooner, but I enjoyed it none the less. Also got one from Viv. Tell him I'll answer "pronto."

Was up to a Masonic Club dance Thursday night. Had a surprisingly good time, but Masons always do. Only trouble our floor was too small. Had a big bunch of girls up from Fredericksburg. There is a Normal school there—a town about the size of Dodge City. Quit about twelve for their train and came down and kidded the sentry enough to not see us go past into camp. —Nit, but got in.

Then on Saturday we drew the guard and I stand so no liberty for Tommy. It got cold as Northern France for our special benefit for it warmed up again today. I had a streak of luck and got the post at the brig guarding prisoners so had it nice. A warm fire and everything, but those on post outside got pretty cold. Was below zero. The southern thermometers didn't register how much

Last week was supposedly our last liberty, so we of course, the guard, were a bit peeved. We are due to "shove off" this week, tho orders so far are only "stand by" so nothing definite, but indications are that we go this time as preparations are being made.

Today I was on police duty and didn't do a blessed thing in the morning; in the afternoon went to a first aid lecture, tho didn't have to, but thot perhaps it wise as a precaution of keeping soul and body together.

Must close this now. Will write again before we leave and of course it may be days or it may be months.

You better take care of yourself and your throat, or they'll have you in the "sick bay" only I guess there is no such thing in the army—whatever they call it anyway.

Tell Viv "hello" and I'll write soon.

Sorry I didn't have more "hat" pictures made. You all seemed to like them best. Most all the boys liked the other and I did too, so I only got a few of them.

TOM.

Letter to Dorto, January 15, 1918

Postmarked Alexandria, VA
"WITH THE COLORS"
YMCA
Jan 15, 1918

Dear Dorto,

I got your dandy letter quite a little while ago & meant
to answer sooner but didn't for some unknown reason.

Was on guard Sunday & it was colder than northern
France. My luck held tho' and I got an inside post so had
no trouble keeping warm. Being on guard tho' beat me out
of the last chance for liberty as we will no doubt leave this
week or at the very latest Sunday. Everything is packed
this time & it really looks like business.

Our lectures have been completed. Finished up with
a couple on first aid. Are learning another new bayonet
manual—will surely be able to handle it when the time
comes. Heinie hates the bayonet too so that's in our favor.

Last Thursday was up to a Mason Club dance uptown.
Most of the ladies from Fredricksburg & had a fine time.
The floor was only too small & the time too short. Had a
nice buffet luncheon, or supper, & then came back & gave
the sentry a stick of candy to let us back in.

The ground & parade ground is a fright. It rains here &
freezes & everything is a sheet of ice & then we live in a
side bill besides. To-day was warmer & it rained last night
so there was about an inch of water all over the ice which
made it especially fine. The major tho' hardly ever minds a
little thing like that so we of course have got to like it.

Mr. Lewis in Washington is a lawyer. Mrs. L. has lived
there always. She is a cousin of Col. Longstreet at present
commanding officer of Camp Jackson in Ga. who is a son,
or grandson, of Gen. Longst. Of Civil War fame. Also she
is well informed on military matters. Her daughter is a

little queen. Just home from boarding school. Have two boys also, one 14, the other about 11. They are both fine lads & the young fellow is mighty interested in everything military.

Must stop now. Present indications are that this will be the last letter from this side. Future address will be 96 Co., 6 th Regt., U. S. Marines, Am. Ex. Forces. The folks will tell you when to start using it as we might not leave as expected. And any mail to the old address will be forwarded. Au revoir & much love to you & also Lucy & Clyde and everyone,

Tom

Letter to Mama, January 16, 1918

Quantico, Va.

Dear Mama:

Got your letter and Bob's and enjoyed them both and also the clippings.

We are working on new bayonet stuff now half the time. The other half, this AM we went down on the river and played shinny on the ice. Would have been swell if we had had skates. Miles and miles of ice and can't skate on it; is a crime for fair.

No drill this PM and no more at all for us here I guess, as we are expected to go Friday, and Sunday at the very latest. Everything is all ready and all we're waiting on now is the good word.

I haven't much news, as I just wrote Vee. I finished my "Laughing Man" tonight and sure liked it. Not much reading now I guess and suppose mail about once a month.

Mrs. Lewis's address is 1669 Thirty first St. Washington, D. C. She certainly is good to us, treats us as if she had known us always, and everything on the place is ours, when we're there.

Has a boy about Ted's age that is quite a lad, sure interested in everything military and has quite a fund of information too.

I'll cut this short as I'll have to hurry up town and get me a hair cut before leaving the old U.S.A.

Will write you again from here.

Lots of love,
TOM.

Letter to Mother, January 17, 1918

Jan. 17, 1918

Dear Mother:

We leave Saturday morning. I write tonight for tomorrow will be a day of inspection and no telling how much time we'll have. Are all packed and our sea-bags will go in the morning and for two or three weeks now we'll live from our packs, and they are mountains too.

Brig. General Lejeune gives troop inspection tomorrow and I suppose it will be certain death for anyone falling under his evil eye, for he's a hard old nut.

Will ship either at Philly or N.Y. Guess it would be unwise to say any more.

I have handed in a card stating "have arrived safely in France." The authorities mail them when we do arrive. Also have given most everyone my address but said you could tell them when to begin using it. It goes into effect now, so write them that whenever you do write to Viv, Helen, Lois, also grannies and Aunt Minnie.

I will write as often and as much as I can from over there, but imagine it will be hard to write an interesting letter that would meet with the approval of the censor, who will be our C.O. I guess.

Had a letter from Ross tonight, also one from Gertrude W. Ross has been in quarantine for measles, didn't have them; seems to be liking the work, tho busy. Can hardly imagine him liking it. I'm afraid he thot I didn't do the square thing by him when we beat it out and joined the Marines. He felt he couldn't up and go like we did and wanted to go with us too. He's infinitely better off where he is, for he's in a company of his old Wichita friends and the C.C. is an old pal of his. Says they haven't their guns yet—that is their six inch guns—and is afraid they won't till they go over.

Gertrude W. has written me some awfully nice letters and I sure appreciate getting them.

Most all the Y.M.C.A. men here are Masons. In fact there are loads of them all over here as well as in the service. I'm sure glad that I got my degrees before I enlisted. Ross said 500 soldiers from Ft. Sill went up to Wichita to take the consistory-32nd.[25] He sure wanted to but said he couldn't afford it. We have some mighty fine men in the company wearing the square and compass. Have four in my bunk house of about 50 men. Would give my hat to sit in a lodge in France but doubt if I could ever prove myself to a Frogeater.

We shall be in training in France no doubt for some time, but we hope to get in on the big show when it opens in the spring.

This war is about 90% pick and shovel and 10% fighting tho; and as "Scotty" says when you dig your "task"—6 ft. and regulation trench depth and width—under fire, it doesn't take long to get it dug. Unfortunately it's always the new guys up there that get bumped off, the old heads

---

25 The consistory 32nd Degree for Masons.

learn it and seem to just keep going no matter what. But in any case as the poilu says "C'est pour France": add to that America and what more could you ask for, even to follow to the "utmost purple rim."

Funny about that island mail, got one from the Bank the same way, but no great difference. Mail from here will be forwarded more easily for organizations are the same.

Love,
Tom.

CHAPTER THREE
OVER THERE

ON THE MORNING OF January 19, 1918, Tom and the 96th Company boarded a train to Philadelphia, Pennsylvania. They traveled to the Navy Yard in the city where they boarded the transport ship, the USS *Henderson*. The *Henderson* set sail to New York Harbor the next day. There the ship and its crew waited for the convoy they would be a part of to assemble. Finally, on the 24th, the *Henderson* set sail with a convoy of four transports and one battleship, the USS *North Carolina*. To avoid submarines, the convoy sailed in a zig-zag pattern as they crossed the Atlantic Ocean. During this trip the Marines were given submarine scanning duties. They were given a schedule of 1 hour on and 8 hours off to scan a given sector of sea with binoculars and report any object to the bridge, even if known. Watching the waves for an hour made Tom seasick and as he says in his memoir, "they saved on my food bill this trip." Luckily, no submarine was encountered during the voyage.

The Marines landed in Europe on February 5, 1918 at the American Expeditionary Force (AEF) Base No. 1 in St. Nazaire, France. On the 8th, the Marines finally disembarked and "marched thru a warehouse loaded with cocoa beans which had a very peculiar odor, which was unpleasant to most of us."[26] The Marines then immediately entrained into the "40 hommes et 8 chevaux" and headed towards the Vosges region.[27] During this ride, Tom mentions in his memoir that, "at our first stop someone asked 'what town is this?' A joker near the door said 'Latrines, France'."

---

26 Excerpt from Tom's memoir.

27 French for "40 men or 8 horses"

The Marines rode the train for three days and three nights in lice-infested cars. Their destination was Damblain, France in the Vosges Mountains, which was a quiet sector.[28] After arriving on the 11th, they marched to Blevaincourt for further training in trench warfare. The Marines were billeted throughout the village. Here they received their combat equipment of steel helmets and gas masks. On February 15, they marched to practice trenches nine miles from the village. The regiment trained mostly at night at Blevaincourt for several weeks enduring freezing temperatures. Tom recalled that, "one night we were over there and it turned bitter cold. We did have our blanket but even so we were on our feet for two on and four off but you might as well be on cause you couldn't sleep, it was too cold."[29] During this period, the Marines were assigned to the 2nd Division and be made into the 4th Brigade.[30]

On March 17th, the Marines hiked to Bourmont where they entrained for Souilly. However, they detrained at Fort Dugny and hiked to Camp Massa, a rear containment camp where units would rotate into or out of the trenches in the Toulon Sector, near Verdun.[31] The train had dropped the Marines off just outside of the German artillery range. Whenever they arrived, the Boche artillery welcomed the 2nd Division with a serenade of shell fire during their hike to Camp Massa.[32] Luckily no one was injured in the barrage.

They remained at the camp, dodging German artillery, until March 28. The 2nd Battalion received orders to relieve the 3rd Battalion at the front lines. The Marines occupied the old Verdun trenches with the 1st, 2nd, and 3rd platoons in the front

---

28 James Carl Nelson, *I Will Hold*, 47.

29 Interview with David Kirk.

30 Nelson, *I Will Hold*, 49.

31 Harrison Cale, "The American Marines at Verdun, Chateau Thierry, Bouresches, and Belleau Wood," *Indiana Magazine of History 15*, no. 2 (June, 1919): 181.

32 Boche is the French word for Germans.

line while the 4th platoon, Tom's platoon, was placed in support trenches at Camp de Bonchamp. Tom mentions in his memoir that it was here they learned how to tell where a shell would land by the sound of it. Unfortunately, being in a support role did not save the 4th platoon from the horror of the war as their position was shelled many times. On April 5, 300 shells fell on the men in a span of one hour. This caused the first casualties from the 96th Company with two privates being killed and two wounded. On the night of April 6, the men were relieved from their duty on the front lines.

From April 7 to 16, the Marines occupied a reserve position at Camp Douzains where they were shelled and attacked with mustard gas which killed two men. From April 17 to 21, the company held the front line at Cotes des Hures and Tresauvaux. While here the Marines held off a German attack, inflicting heavy casualties. Then from April 22 to 23, they occupied a reserve position at Camp Chifoure. From April 24 to 30, they were again on the front lines near Ronvaux.

At some point during this time at the front, Tom was assigned to reconnaissance duty into No Man's Land. In an interview with his grandson, David Kirk, he mentions his duty and thoughts on it.

> You were facing their trenches and they were facing our trenches and every night there would be a patrol go out to try and see if they were making any changes or anything. One thing that always bothered me a little bit, this patrol was not supposed to open fire on anybody, but you were supposed to get back into your trenches as fast as you could and report what you found out. And in my mind I always thought, here we come tearing back, these guys are gonna think we're heinies and shoot us but they never did.[33]

---

33 Tom's interview with David Kirk.

Tom also received a shrapnel wound in the small of his back while on the front, later saying, "If it had been larger and gone in deeper, you folks probably would have had a gold star in your service flag."

Finally, the Marines were relieved from duty on the front on May 1 to 12.[34] They then travelled a long journey to about 25 miles northwest of Paris near the French villages of Gisors and Chaumont-en-Vexin drilling, maneuver training, and resting. During their time on the front, the 96th Company had suffered casualties of five men killed and twelve wounded.

Letter to Mother, January 21, 1918

Aboard Ship.

Dear Mother:

Am well and fine so far and do feel much as if I would be sea sick.

It is cold as can be where we are. Have no idea how many degrees below zero but feels like plenty. Plow thru broken ice nearly all the time.

You should see our Pullman quarters, sure keen, I say, but about what I had expected.

Chow is good but have to fight almost to get it, and have no place to eat it.

Must close this.

Lots of love,
Tom.

---

34 *History of the 96th Company*. This applies for all dates in this chapter previously listed.

Letter to Mother, February 12, 1918

Somewhere in France

Dear Mother:

It seems ages since I last wrote you and I hope you haven't worried. However at last we are settled enough so we can write letters again. I could have written from the boat but thot that it would reach you about as soon to wait until we landed.

The censorship is even more strict than they tell us in the states and there is almost nothing about the country or ourselves that we are allowed to write.

Everything has been splendid so far & mostly more than up to our expectations and of course many things different from what we had expected.

It is surely a pretty country and quaint scenes. Houses are all built for centuries, made of stone and stucco and in the newer ones some tile is used, tied in and trimmed at the corners with white stones or red brick. Red tile roofs almost entirely.

Spring is much earlier here than at home and it seems quite mild to what most of us expected. Very damp and water is no good, which I suppose accounts for the French being such wine drinkers. There is, of course, plenty of sterilized water for the army.

Guess I can't tell anything about our ocean trip, unless that we did not have very rough weather; after about two days out tho, I got "mal de mer" and it stuck with me for about a week, and I sure swore then I'd stay here the rest of my life or walk back.[35]

Was not so cold at sea, but man, the wind! Western Kansas isn't in it.

---

35 "mal de mer" means seasickness.

I got a letter today from Lois that was sent to Paris Island about the first of Sept. Guess it has been lying around over here ever since. Incoming and outgoing mail both is censored. Soldier mail free to the states or camps in France.

Haven't gotten on to speaking French so well yet, that I have forgotten my English. Have met a couple of old Island bunkies who came over some time ago. Nothing of any of the boys from home tho.

There are thousands of things I'd like to tell you all about, but think no use to try, so will close now. Will write soon tho, there will no doubt be little to say except, "I am well," I suppose. Mails may be delayed or lost so don't worry if you don't hear from me, for I shall write regularly unless for some reason I can't. No news is always good news, for you will be notified if anything is wrong ever.

Lots of love,
Tom.

O.K. Lt. C. B. Cates

Letter to Mother, February 18, 1918

Dear Mother:

Have been here long enough now to get started out on our work pretty well. The company is quarantined for mumps, but I guess I'm safe. I've had them once and been around them enough to have them again if I am to have them again. We can't go to the "Y" tho now, or any place like that.

We are within hearing distance of the big guns here, which ought to make us work hard I guess.

This last week has been colder than usual for here, they say, but dry, so we don't mind the cold for the benefit of having a little sunshine and dry weather.

Some mail came in a few days ago, but I haven't been lucky yet. Guess I'll get a letter next time.

Floyd B. was over to see us yesterday and gave us some Hutchinson papers, but they were Jan. 1 and of course we left the states after that. We get Paris editions of a couple of American papers here tho, so we are not clear out of the world.

It is hard to write a letter any more; so much to say and so little that can be said.

I am getting along fine in every way.

Hope you are all well.

Tom.

O. K. LT. C. B. Cates

Letter to Dorothy, February 22, 1918

Dear Dorothy,

Your letter came last night in our first mail from the states & I was sure glad to hear from you. I didn't get any mail from home but guess they are all well.

Had a dandy trip of course & mighty interesting but can't tell much about it. We came up here in little French box cars about one-fourth the size of ours and have been pretty busy up here ever since. To-day is a holiday so am writing a few letters, washing clothes, etc.

You sure are doing well with your savings stamps and your knitting. I have plenty of everything knitted so don't send me any. Some day when you are trying out your domestic science tho you might send some cake or candy.

Pretty soft for you getting out of all your quizzes and everything. Guess you are having an old time winter there. Is the coal still as scarce?

There is not much we can write about so I will stop for now.

Lots of love,
Tom

96th Co., 2nd Batt. 6th Regt.
U.S.M.C. A.E.F.

OK Lt. C. B. Cates

Letter to Mother, March 9, 1918

Dear Mother,

I got your letter written Feb. 9th a day or so ago. I guess you hadn't gotten the card yet? Did you ever get my letter I mailed from aboard ship? You should have several letters by this time and should they come irregular don't worry about me, for I'll be all right.

That is quite a shock to Mrs. Krom and certainly sudden. I guess Mrs. Cavernaugh had been pretty sick for a long time.

That guy up in the house at Spearville must be a dope for fair. He certainly has messed up enough. Is there still a coal shortage out there? Pretty hard on flowers if you can't get the coal to keep the furnace going, isn't it. Haven't gotten the package yet but doubtless will in the next mail.

Paul sure doesn't know a good thing when he has it, that's all, he will some day tho!

We are having nice weather here now. I haven't much to tell you, there is so little we can write.

Lots of love,
Tom

OK Lt. C.B. Cates

Letter to Mother, March 23, 1918

AMERICAN Y.M.C.A.
On Active Service With the American Expeditionary
Force

Dear Mother,

Was sure glad to get letters from all of you and also
got the Hersheys and believe me you couldn't have sent
anything more welcome than 'American' chocolate.

Got letters from you folks & also Lois, Helen, Viv & the
folks at Spearville. I won't be able to answer them, I fear,
so when I do write, you'll have to pass them around & I'll
write to you as often as possible & to the rest if I should
be that lucky.

Am still doing fine here and getting along all right, so
above all don't worry over me even if you don't hear for
I'll be all right. Our mail comes irregular — got some late
mail & this later older, so perhaps yours will come this
same way.

Must close this; am well; love to everybody and many,
many thanks for the candy.

Tom

E. A. Harris

Letter to Mother, April 2, 1918

Dear Mother,

It has been quite a while since I wrote last but this is
not the States over here. I got a bunch of letters last week.
One of yours written the 8th of last month after you had
heard from me. I am glad you at least are leaving tho it's
not much I can write.

Stanley is still with me but I don't get to see him
very often. Tell Po and Em he is engaged to a girl in Os.

since along in the winter so they needn't bemoan his broken heart over Blanche. Got 3 letters from V written 3 consecutive weeks. I'll write her soon. Glad Helen did so well. I'm proud of her. I suppose tho' she is disappointed not getting first.

Tell Viv he is to take the Colo. job absolutely not the 'other'. Poor Jesse W.L. I was tickled when I heard he had enlisted for I doubted if he'd get out of his 'boot camp'.

Floyd S. and the Hill's boys are not so far from us now but haven't gotten to see any of them.

Sure is dandy about Uncle Clint's offer. You've simply got to make Dad take it up. I don't see how he could keep it anyway. Let Viv take the greenhouse. The responsibility will do him good.

Must close this now.

Lots and lots of love to everybody,
Tom

Ok. Lt. C.B.Cates

Mailing Card to Mother, April 16, 1918

Dear Mother,

Am well. Will write soon.

Tom

OK. C.B. Cates
2nd Lieut. U.S.M.C.

Letter to Mother, May 4, 1918

Somewhere in France

Dear Mother:

I should have written long before this but it simply could not be done. Have been up in the trenches for some time as you may already have guessed; since a few days after my birthday.

Have had quite a bit of shell fire, a little gas and plenty of excitement of various kinds but am still in one piece so far. The trenches are surely muddy, knee deep in many places; have running water in the dugouts and water knee deep in some of the bomb proofs.

Have been able to keep clear of the 'cooties' so far, but we not only eat and sleep with the rats, but at night on watch they throw rocks at you from the parapet. They are certainly familiar.

They sure said truly when the guy said "give me the safety of the front line" but there are disadvantages to it even with all its "safety." It is pretty hard to get up such things as water and 'chow'!! We went a long time without hearing from anyone but not long ago got a lot of mail including the picture. I knew about the 'embargo' on soldiers' packages so I don't know whether I'll even get any of those or not. Here's hoping.

Am surely glad to hear that granny is getting along so fine. You must tell her I'll write if I can get a chance. You folks in Larned have gotten every letter I've been able to write so far, so tell Helen & Lois not to be peeved. I have gotten a couple of dandy letters from them both but simply haven't had a chance to answer.

Guess Freddy will like it better now, he is at his photography again.[36] I wish I had been there to take advantage of his studio, I'd sure 'horn in' on his dark room. There is surely a lot of pretty country here and it is a shame we can't take pictures. I sure wish you did have some of our rains there. Until this week I hadn't seen dry dirt in France.

---

36 Fred Merrick, Tom's Uncle, married to Aunt "Po".

Glad Viv is going out to Florence, Colorado. It's the finest thing he can do.

We get practically no news of the war here and keep wondering how it's all going. Tell Vera it never 'quits' raining here. Some western Kansas dust would sure look good to me.

Never expect to see Bob Hood, or Red, or the Hill boys after I see the situation here. Stanley is still with us. I don't see him often tho. He says tell you 'hello' when I write.

Please thank Po, Emmie, and Harry for the Smileage books, tho doubt whether I ever use them over here. Also thank Helen for the 'Van Dyke.' It is certainly splendid and congratulate her for me if I can't write before Commencement.

Love,
Tom.

O. K. LT. C. B. Cates

Letter to Dad, May 8, 1918

Dear Dad:

I think I'd better write you even tho I just wrote mama a day or so ago. These chances to write are by fits and starts, and so don't you folks worry if you don't hear from me for awhile; for you'll just know I can't write.

I wrote and told you I got the picture. It is dandy. I haven't gotten the package yet but guess it is much slower in getting thru. I sent a request in the last letter, tho forgot to say anything about it. If it hasn't gone when you get this, put in a small jar of mentholatum. Have been getting all your letters and think tho they come in bunches as perhaps mine do to you.

I told about all I could of what we do and are doing in my last letter. We keep on the go pretty well so that means lots of hiking and we've been carrying a full pack—all our worldly goods.

We had a good thunder & lightning storm last night, about the first we've had. Didn't seem natural not to hear the 'whistle' of the shell when you hear the crack and see the flash. Did seem more like a Kansas storm tho. My bunk is open on one side so it is sure outdoor life; last night the wind blew some but we escaped a soaking.

Your 'menu' sounds mighty good to me in spite of Mr. Hoover. The milk, eggs, and cornbread sure listen good to me. Our regular bill is bacon and spuds for breakfast; beef and spuds for dinner, and stew & rice for supper; coffee & bread at each meal, and that is all, provided the Hun artillery does not locate our 'chow' house.

Too bad things are looking so bad around Spearville. Had a letter from Emma the other day. She says they are sure up against it. Glad granny is getting better all the time, tho is pretty hard for Em at best. Mama wrote about the Weidowers; they are sure having a time of it. Glad mama can get up to granny's so often. Too bad Jr. broke his arm. He seems to be having his share of bad luck.

Tell Vera my memory is not of the best, so I would hesitate to contradict any of Bee T.'s statements, but sure can say she has a very remarkable imagination for one so young. I may have met her Hutchinson friend. But I sure didn't meet him in Paris or any other city in France or England. Give her my kindest regards when you see her at any rate, and tell her yes, I met all her friends.

We changed time over here March 1. But such a matter makes only a little difference for we draw as much duty at night as day.

Got Viv's letter the other day and was glad to hear from him. Also had one from Nina and she was sure tickled that he was coming out. He'll have a good time there all right. Nina also said Dick Burgess sent his regards. Also had a nice letter from Aunt Minnie. Don't know when I'll get a chance to answer any of my letters.

When you go up to Spearville next time get a First National Bank statement and send it when you write. Is Florence W. still with them?

Signed the pay roll today. They told us in the states everything was cheap over here and we wouldn't need money. Everything isn't cheap but money is no use for there is no place to spend it.

Must close this now.

Lots of love to everybody.
Tom.

Letter to Tom from Granny, May 10, 1918

My Dear Tom,

I wonder what you are doing today. Have not heard from you for two weeks & Vernon don't hear from Stanley very often. Vernon is a pretty lonely boy these days, comes to see us quite often. He and Emma went to Dodge Tuesday eve to hear some Camp Funston boys who gave an entertainment there.[37] Said it was good, saw them put on their gas masks.

It is very cool today. I have a fire in the grate, was real warm first of the week. I heard from your mother last eve. They were all well. I think I will go to Larned tomorrow to see Frederick.[38] He was up here over last Sunday. The country looks swell now, the wheat coming out better than expected.

---

37 Emma is Tom's aunt.

38 Frederick is Tom's uncle.

I did not get this letter finished Friday; it is now Monday & I am out on the porch writing & most lovely morning. Emma & I have been alone since Friday the first time since I have not been well. I had the first letter you wrote to me printed in Spearville paper but the editor was so slow he only printed it a couple weeks ago so many people spoke of the letter, how glad they were to read your letter, it was so interesting, etc. Vernon was here last eve, he said he had a letter from Stanley; said he had been in the trenches, etc. I don't like to think of you being there, but I knew we must expect most anything in war. You are fighting for the liberty of the world, surely a just and righteous cause. God will surely be with you to keep & protect you. The Psalmist says, "A thousand shall fall at thy side & a thousand at thy right hand but it shall not come nigh thee."

It seems to me we can see a little light breaking through the clouds now, but I may be mistaken. I do hope & pray that the end is near. Vernon is very restless & wants to be doing some war work too. Jessie Lantry is still in California. Bettie W. still in NewPresst. at work. Ed Weidower is to leave today for some camp. We are to have another Red Cross drive soon. People are denying themselves & giving freely to the war funds. We must all do our bit to win the war. Yesterday was Mother's day. Your folks sent me some nice flowers. I suppose they had a busy time. The girls will write you soon. Hope to hear from you soon.

Much love from,
Grannie

Letter to Mother, May 24, 1918

Dear Mother:

It has been quite a while since I last wrote, but I am
doing my best. There was quite a bit of publicity about
Mother's Day letters for soldiers but we didn't get a
chance to get ours out for reasons you may guess.

We have sure had lots of hiking since I last wrote
and are now back of the lines for a while and are surely
putting in a day's work. Schedule starts at 5:30 AM and
we are sure busy till taps at 9:30 PM

We have had a few summer days here but today it
seems like winter again almost. The part of France I have
seen in the last week has improved my opinion of it quite
a lot.

Came very near getting a chance to see 'Al' if that is the
name of Bee's friend in Paris.

It is surely nice to get a rest from the 'sighing Susies'
'Whistling Bills' etc., but I'm afraid we don't appreciate it
or it is simply in-bred in a soldier to 'crab.'

Bob Hood is in my division over here tho I never have
seen him or anyone from his regiment. It seems funny
that as long as I have been so close to him both in the
states and here, I haven't been able to see him.

I got the box all right about a week ago. The cake was
sure fine and came thru in the best of condition. Also
the gloves were absolutely O.K. tho pretty good ones for
a buck private. Many, many thanks for everything. We
are not supposed to carry any knit goods, so I gave the
wristlets to a French kid.

Have never seen Hill nor any of those but have followed
on their trail a week or so behind. We have fought on,
perhaps, the most noted sector of the whole war.

Vera asks if we are doing patrol duty. Yes, but mostly in
No Man's Land. None back of the lines.

Don't worry about us now tho, for we're out of the range, at least for a while.

Must close this for now,

Lots of love,
Tom.

Letter to Mother, May 26, 1918

Somewhere in France

Dear Mother:

Got your letter and dad's yesterday and also today, Vera's, and was sure glad for them all; also got one from granny and Em. You'll have to keep them posted when I don't get to write them.

Was glad to see Red's letter which was interesting. As for excitement, I guess, I have him skinned a little. At one time, when we were up in the trenches, I lived five days out in "no man's land" without going back as far as the first line. We got two shellings in the five days there, so were glad to get out when we did.

Aeroplanes are about the most common things there are when it is clear. In the very first bombardment we were in, I got a very small shell fragment, which I carried around for about a day before I realized what it was. Was going to send it to you but the hospital corpsman lost it.

Tell Ted I can't think of any dogs as Red did. Perhaps you can guess the sector we were on from my oldest sister's name. Drop the first letter from my third sister's name and guess where I am now, tho behind the front. We went thru the outskirts of the town "Red" saw the sights in, in our box cars last week. We didn't see much.

We are supposed to be soldiers now, I guess. When we were inspected not long ago by Gen. Pershing he asked if

there were any recruits in our company. The answer was
"No."

We are sure hitting the ball here, hard enough to make
us think the real rest billets are in the front line. We are
billeted in barns here. I'm up in a loft. Lots of straw and
straw lice but better than the cement floors and cobble
stones we had for a few days on the hikes coming to this
place. It is no trouble at all to capture "cooties," but I'm
afraid they would not flourish on American climate.

Listen if you can't get Viv back in school this fall
and he insists on "going in," make him enlist in the
ambulance corps. He's got no business going for a couple
of years yet tho.

This is a typical little French town, we are in here. No
streets except a couple of main ones. The rest run into
squares with buildings all around them. There is nothing
to buy in town—no stores. A café of course but no beer.
Champagne too high here and their "vin" is rotten. The
last town we were in champagne was only 5 ½ francs
when we came, and only 7 when we left—maybe you
think they didn't sell some.

Take the first syllable of my youngest sister's name and
guess it. We were the first American troops there tho.
Prices are always higher after the first bunch has been in a
town. Also we had a pay day there. That is quite an event
over here.

I haven't seen a paper since the middle of April, so
know nothing about the war or anything. Granny sent a
bank statement for Dec. last. Said Harry wouldn't send
a later one. I saw a Ford County Bank one in April, tho. I
guess things are none too promising.

Everything here looks fine and the country, as Red says,
looks more like Kansas, only it is much more intensively
cultivated. Well, I must close this now. Hope you and dad
enjoyed the "Messiah" as I know you did.

Much love to everybody,
Tom

Letter to Doc, May 26, 1918

Dear Doc:

I've gotten both your letters and this is the first chance I've had to answer. We are back of the lines again for a short while and are sure hitting the ball from 5:30 to 9:30 PM so we think our rest billet is at the front, not the rear. But at that I haven't heard anyone wishing for the front line. It is some relief to be out of range of the 'sighing Susies.'

Am not so far away from 'BO,' if what we hear is true, but doubt if I ever see him. Bob Hood is in my division and I have never seen him nor any of his company, so you see how it is.

I passed thru the town Bee Taylor's friend is in last week, but hadn't before and only thru the edge this time so didn't see much.

There are plenty of chickens there but none here. This is a village of perhaps a thousand in peace time and we are billeted in barns, but have some straw even if it is lousy and sure feels good, along side of the cement floors we slept on when on the hike, before getting here.

This is a good country here and the crops are fine and every inch is under cultivation, sure looks pretty.

Do you ever see Dick Burgess there? Tell him 'Bonjour' for me when you do. You surely want to go over to Colo. Springs before you go back. It is sure one good town in the summer time.

Tell Nina I got her letter and will answer when I can. This letter writing is sure a proposition over here. The only way is just not write and I've sure come pretty nearly doing that.

When do you go to training camp? Believe me you're sure foolish if you enlist before you're 21 and at least you've got no business in it at 18.

I see Jess and Ed. W. are trying the Marines. I expected they would be drafted.

Well I must close this for now. Give my love to the whole family out there.

Yours,
Tom.

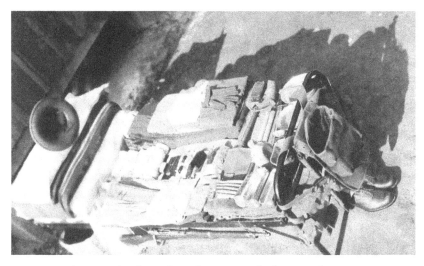

Photograph taken of "Junk on an Bunk" by Pvt. Thomas L. Stewart, Complete Uniform and Equipment issued to Pvt. Thomas L. Stewart, Paris Island, South Carolina, in 1917.

Photograph taken of Barracks "Field Day" by Pvt. Thomas L. Stewart, Co H. Recruit Barracks, Marine Barracks, Paris Island, South Carolina, on September 1917.

Author's Note: The photos in this section are 100 years old and very small in their original form. Therefore, given their age and condition, the reprint quality is less than ideal. However, for those interested, you can see clearer versions of them online on the Facebook page "The Story of One Marine."

Photograph taken by Pvt. Thomas L. Stewart of the Paris Island
Rifle Range. Paris Island, South Carolina, 1917.

Photograph taken of Pvt. Thomas L. Stewart,
Paris Island, South Carolina, 1917.

Photograph taken of barbed wire obstacle by Pvt. Thomas L. Stewart at Quantico, September 1917.

Photograph taken of Pvt. Thomas L. Stewart(left) and Stanley R. Williams(right) in front of the National Capital Building on October 8th, 1917.

Photograph taken of Pvt. Thomas L. Stewart in the practice trenches at Quantico, Virginia on September 30th, 1917.

Photograph taken by Pvt. Thomas L. Stewart of Stanley R. Williams (left) and an unknown Marine in the practice trenches at Quantico, Virginia on September 30, 1917.

Photograph taken by Pvt. Thomas L. Stewart of Stanley R. Williams (right) and an unknown Marine at the practice trenches at Quantico, Virginia on September 30, 1917.

Photograph taken by Pvt. Thomas L. Stewart of Edgar C. Seik (left) and two unknown Marines at Quantico, Virginia in September 1917.

Photograph taken of Pvt. Thomas L. Stewart on top of an 155mm
Training Howitzer at Quantico, Virginia in November 1917.

*Photograph taken of Pvt. Thomas L. Stewart in his
uniform at Quantico, Virginia in December 1917.*

Photograph taken after the Battle of the Aisne (Belleau Wood) of the destroyed French village of Bouresches, France where the 96th Co (H). 6th Marine Regiment along with the 79th Co (F). fought on the evening of Thursday, June 6th, 1918.

Photograph taken by Pvt. Thomas L. Stewart of Camp Rochambeau, France, outside of Tours, France in February 1919.

*Photograph taken by Pvt. Thomas L. Stewart of the Commander
of American Expeditionary Forces, John J. Pershing and the United
States Secretary of War, Newton D. Baker as they inspect the
American University at Beaune, France in April 1919.*

Photograph taken by Pvt. Thomas L. Stewart of
French locals near Beaune, France, in May 1919.

*Photograph taken by Pvt. Thomas L. Stewart of two
unknown soldiers while visiting the ancient roman aqueduct
near Lyon, France on May 20th, 1919.*

Photograph taken by Pvt. Thomas L Stewart of the
Beaune Cathedral in May, 1919.

Photograph taken by Pvt. Thomas L. Stewart of the American
occupied Castle Arenfels in Bad Honningen, Germany in June 1919.

*Photograph taken by Pvt. Thomas L. Stewart, with
two unknown Marines at the French Alps near
Chamonix-Mont-Blanc, France in June, 1919.*

Photograph taken of Pvt. Thomas L. Stewart (in front) with unknown Marine while in the Place de la Concorde, Paris, France in June 1919.

*Photograph taken by Pvt. Thomas L. Stewart of Marines from the
96th Co (H). 6th Marine Regiment as they had their uniforms
cleaned from a Delouser, aka The "Cootie Wagon" at the 3rd U.S.
Army Railhead at Koblenz, Germany, taken in July, 1919.*

*Photograph taken by Pvt. Thomas L. Stewart of Marines from the
2nd Battalion, 6th Marine Regiment as they watch an Inter-Battalion
boxing tournament on the aft deck of the USS Washington, while on
the voyage back to the United States in July 1919.*

Photograph taken by Pvt. Thomas L. Stewart of Marines from the
96th Co (H). 6th Marine Regiment as they prepare to leave the
3rd U.S. Army Railhead at Koblenz, Germany in July 1919.

Photograph taken of Pvt. Thomas L. Stewart
upon his return home in in August, 1919.

CHAPTER FOUR
BOURESCHES

THE TRAINING AND REST did not last long. On May 30, orders
were issued for the 2nd Division to relieve the 1st Division at
Cantigny. However, the next day, orders were changed to relieve
the French army at Chateau-Thierry. The Marines then boarded
trucks and rushed to reinforce the French. The German Army
had pushed a new offensive that had demolished the French and
British armies, creating a bulge in the Allied line fifteen miles
deep and forty miles wide.[39] The Germans were now only 35 miles
from Paris.[40] The Marines rode for a full 30 hours through hordes
of fleeing French villagers who looked upon the Americans with
hope that the Germans would finally be stopped.[41] During this
time, from May 30 to June 16, Tom did not write a single letter
home so I will fill in the gap in his account.

On June 1, the 2nd Battalion disembarked from the trucks
in the village of Montreuil at 4:00 AM[42] The men rested and ate
their first meal in 30 hours. The 96th Company then moved
towards the American line along the Paris-Metz Highway. They
occupied the line north of the highway, dug holes for protection, and waited for the Germans. Meanwhile, the French army
retreated from their position running through the American
lines, making the Marines the new front for the defense of Paris.
Then, on June 2, the remaining French soliders came running
towards the Americans warning that the Germans were right
behind them. An artillery barrage announced the attack as the

---

39 Nelson, *I Will Hold*, 66.

40 Ibid.

41 Harrison Cale, 185.

42 *History of the 96th Company*, 50.

Germans came swarming through the wheat fields on the heels of the retreating troops.

The Germans, confident in victory, charged the field in mass formation. However, they were not expecting to encounter the American Marines. As they charged, machine guns raked their numbers. The Marines also took the time to sight in their rifles before firing. Most of them had at least a 'Marksmen' badge and some qualified as 'Sharpshooter' and 'Expert Rifleman', which culminated to a stonewall defense.[43] The Germans continued to push until their casualties became too great and they fell back into the woods. Private Orley Dunton, who was also part of the 96th Company, recalled that:

> The boys did not simply raise their rifles and shoot in the general direction of Germany. They adjusted their sights, coolly took aim and shot to kill. I cannot believe that one shot in ten missed a mark. The Prussians dropped as if Death were wielding his scythe in their midst, rank after rank.[44]

The Americans faced the German Crown Prince's own army of hardened veterans and elite shock troops. But for the first time in their offensive, the Germans had been stopped.

For the next three days, the Marines waited for another attack that never came. Instead, the artillery, from both sides, laid down constant, heavy bombardment. While lying low, the Marines were forced to eat their emergency rations as they could not get food for the first 60 hours.[45] During this time, the 96th suffered nine casualties.[46]

---

43 Nelson, *I Will Hold*, 78.

44 Orley Dunton, "Mussing Up The Prussian Guard," *Hearst's Magazine*, December, 1918, 488.

45 Nelson, 79.

46 Ibid.

On the night of June 5, the men were relieved from the line. The next day, June 6, they moved to a position in the northwest corner of the Bois de Clerembouts, near la Cense Farm. The members of the company then spent the day trying to catch some sleep and constructing crosses and fences for fallen soldiers. According to First Lieutenant Clifton B. Cates, most of the men believed the company had moved to the rear to get a rest.[47] At 4:30 PM orders came that the 96th was tasked with retaking the town of Bouresches, which had been taken by the Germans on June 2.[48]

On June 6, the plan was that Major Berton Sibley's 3rd Battalion, 6th Marine Regiment would advance from the area around Lucy-le-Bocage and move east. The left side of Major Sibley's battalion would sweep though the southern edge of Belleau Wood in an effort to connect with Major Benjamin Berry's 3rd Battalion, 5th Marine Regiment, who were attacking the wood directly from the east. Meanwhile the right half of Sibley's Battalion moved parallel to the road that ran from Lucy-le-Bocage to Bouresches. The 2nd Battalion, 6th Marine Regiment, under Major Thomas Holcomb, was tasked to meet with the right flank of Major Sibley's battalion and attack Bouresches directly.[49]

Major Holcomb assigned the 96th Company to attack the town. The 79th Company was to support the 96th's assault. The company had moved into Clerembauts Wood about a mile south of Bouresches before the attack. At 4:30 PM, 30 minutes before the attack was to commence, orders went out to the company commanders. Major Holcomb recalled that they received orders at 4:55PM that stated the Second Battalion would go over the top at 5:05 PM. This gave them only 10 minutes to issue the or-

---

47 Kevin Seldon, "The Battle of Belleau Wood: America's Indoctrination into 20th Century Warfare" (master's thesis, University of Central Oklahoma, 2010), 131.

48 *History of the 96th Company*, 51.

49 Kevin Seldon, 117-118.

ders and move into position.[50] The 96th Company had to cover half a mile in 10 minutes to be in position to begin the assault. The Marines made it to their starting position in time for the attack to begin.

The 3rd Battalion began their attack at 5:00 PM. As they crossed the fields, fire from hidden machine gun nests in Belleau Wood decimated their ranks. The Marines filed into the ranks of the fallen and continued pushing towards their objective. Heavy losses ensued as they attempted to fight towards Bouresches. This led the battalion to break from their objective. Instead, the survivors found what little cover they could in the tree line of Belleau Wood and began looking for the hidden machine guns.[51]

As the 3rd Battalion fought along the wood, the 96th prepared for their assault on the town. The Company advanced in a formation where each platoon made up four skirmish lines. The men had to cross an open wheat field more than 200 yards wide.[52] Enemy machine guns from the tree-line of Belleau Wood and from the town began working over the ranks of Marines as they emerged through the wheat and several men in the first waves fell wounded. Corporal Glen Hill watched the advance from the seclusion of a shell hole and wrote in a letter home that, "As they were crossing the field you could see the exploding shells and incessant whine of machine gun bullets and the men dropping along the way."[53]

The Company's Captain, Donald Duncan advanced with the right flank. Smoking a straight-stemmed pipe and carrying a cane. But moments later an enemy round tore through his abdomen and the thirty-five-year old captain slumped to the ground. Immediately, First Sergeant Aloysius Sheridan and Peter C. Ward ran to his aid, followed by First Sergeant Joseph Sissler

---

50 Ibid, 131.

51 Ibid, 130.

52 Harrison Cale, *The American Marines*, 187.

53 As cited by Seldon, 134.

and Lieutenant Junior Grade Weedon Osborne. They ran over and helped move Captain Duncan to shelter. The men reached a nearby tree line but as soon as they laid the Captain on the ground, a shell landed directly on them, killing all but Sheridan and Ward.[54] The loss of the Captain left First Lieutenant James Robertson in charge of the company.

The enemy guns situated in the town laid waste to the first wave of the 96th Company. According to Second Lieutenant Joseph C. Grayson of the 79th Company, most of the first wave of the battalion fell dead or wounded within the first three minutes of the assault.[55] Tom's platoon, 4th platoon, under Second Lieutenant Clifton B. Cates, was on the right edge of the 96th Company and formed skirmish lines, keeping up a running fire until being pinned to the ground.[56] They fought in the American style of advancing, in short rushes and then diving to the ground for cover. The bullets whipped and cut their clothing as the machine gun fire was so thick that Tom swore, in a later letter, that it was "a perfect hailstorm of machine gun bullets. Had anyone told me a person could live in it, I'd have laughed at him." It was during this attack that Tom's friend Stanley was hit in the shoulder by a machine gun bullet and evacuated. Robertson, now in command, saw the danger facing the company as they laid exposed in the field and stood up among the bullets waving his pistol in the air in order to get everyone's attention. He signaled for the remnants of the company to follow him into the ravine along the right side of the field. The survivors of the 4th Platoon began to maneuver to their right towards Robertson. During this maneuver to the ravine, Cates was struck in the helmet by a machine gun bullet, knocking him unconscious.[57]

---

54 *History of the 96th*, 27.

55 Grayson, *A Record of the Operations of the Second Battalion*. National Archives, Washington, D.C.

56 Seldon, 136.

57 Ibid.

Tom and the survivors of the company crawled across the machine gun swept and artillery barraged field to the ravine and followed Robertson into the town. Tom mentions in his memoir that, "knowing the road would be defended we went over a six foot stone wall and took possession [of the town]." Tom also recalled in his interview with David Kirk,

> We made sure there were no more Germans in
> the town, they fled from us. When we counted up
> and we had 26 men and our lieutenant was not
> with us but he came on a little bit later. He had
> sustained a machine gun bullet that hit his helmet
> and knocked him out cold. I always thought it took
> a bit of guts when he got up, he came to, and his
> company was not in sight, we were in the town.
> He came on forward instead of going back.

Indeed Cates did rejoin his men after regaining consciousness, bringing other Marines he encountered in the ravine, and took over for Robertson, who left to get reinforcements.[58]

Cates led the men as they captured the village. Upon entering the western part of town, the Marines engaged in fierce, close quarters combat. Bouresches was occupied by over one hundred Germans with machine gun emplacements all throughout the town, including the church steeple.[59] The men fought house to house as they tossed grenades into buildings, chasing the Germans from their strongholds and out of town. The Marines fiercely battled through the machine gun fire until they were on top of the German positions. Tom mentions that "if in a tight place, it's 'Kamerad.'[60] But it's hard to hear them when they've been cutting you to pieces with machine guns." The Germans

---

58 Seldon, 149.

59 Harrison Cale. 187.

60 German term meaning "friend" used to indicate surrender.

finally fled the town but positioned machine guns along the road, halting the Marine advance.

The Marines now faced the task of holding onto Bouresches. Only a handful of Marines had made it into the town as night fell. Luckily reinforcements arrived in the evening, but the force in town was still severely understrength. To counter this, Cates had his men constantly change position and fire to make it seem like there were more men in town.[61] The men also faced the problem of having outpaced their kitchen and were forced to eat their emergency rations. Tom shared some French bread he had hoarded away with Cates during their first night. The Germans then gave the men a terrific shelling that night. Tom mentions in his memoir, "that morning I reached out of my foxhole to see an unexploded 75 mm shell lying there. It was tenderly disposed of." During the severe shelling the first night, Tom acted as a runner for Cates. Stanley Williams mentions this in a letter home.

Letter to Merle Ward from Stanley Williams excerpt, September 26, 1918

...You ask about Majors Holcomb and Sibley, both of our regiment, and Holcomb has our battalion. Capt. Duncan was our company captain and Robertson first lieutenant who took charge when Duncan was killed and led the 24 men into the town Vernon sent you a clipping about. Tom was one of the 24, and so was Dunlavy you asked about. Tex, as we called him took a German machine gun single handed and won a D.S.O., only to be killed two days later.

If you haven't yet write to Tom and insist on a complete description of that battle for he was right in the thickest of it and had the most dangerous job, "liason" or runner, carrying orders from one company to another and keeping connections which was very essential to holding a

---

61 Nelson, 101.

position. You know how modest he is, anyway, but to me he admitted he had quite a thrilling experience, running right into a German outpost and getting away without getting plugged...

For the next three days, the Germans continuously bombarded the village and attempted small raids into the town to no avail. The Marines held onto Bouresches through the constant artillery until June 10 when they were finally relieved by members of the 5th Marine Regiment. The surviving members of the company marched to a support position south of Lucy-le-Bocage at La Mon Blanche.[62]

While in reserve, Tom helped carry wounded from the frontlines. The Marines then rested for three days and nights until June 13 when they were ordered to Belleau Wood in preparation for a German counterattack.[63] At 5:30 PM, the 96th Company was ordered into the woods to relieve the 2nd Battalion, 5th Regiment. When night fell, the men prepared to enter the Bois de Belleau. However, before they could enter, shells began falling on their position. The shells released mustard gas throughout the wood. The Marines quickly reached for their gas masks and dug in. For the next five hours between 6000 to 7000 shells of high explosive, gas, and airburst rained down on the men.[64] The men were caught in the heaviest bombardment they had ever encountered. They all gave in to the urge to hunker down and wait out the bombardment. Unfortunately, the poisonous gas filled the air and seeped into their clothing.

As the men tried to retreat to a safer position, the volume of shells created a daunting wall that the Marines needed to cross in order to reach a safer position. Harrison Cale recalled that the shells "were falling on the path to the road about every six

---

62 Nelson, 120.

63 Ibid.

64 Ibid, 121-22

seconds. This obliged us to time the shells by counting off the seconds and sending the men through the barrage on the run, starting them while pieces of the exploded shells were still flying in the air."[65]

All down the line, Marines were forced to evacuate in the darkness while being hindered by their gas masks and the constant danger around them. Cale continues his account by stating "the woods was a mass of crashing shells and falling trees as the gas, mingled with high explosives, swept through the branches."[66]

In the daylight of June 14, the Marines finally evacuated the wounded. The Marines who had kept their gas masks on still suffered from the gas. It had seeped into their clothing and, since it was a hot summer night, the oily gas reacted with the sweat causing burns all over their bodies. Tom was one of the Marines fortunate enough to remain standing after the attack but on the 15th, he, Cates, and the other remaining Marines were forced to evacuate to the field hospital for aid. Tom was evacuated back to Base Hospital 17 in Dijon, France.

The price of the last 15 days was great on the 96th Company. In all, they had suffered 39 killed and 269 wounded.[67] But, they had stopped the German advance toward Paris, taken Bouresches, and held onto it until reinforcements arrived. Their actions brought them fame and glory from both the Allies and Germany. The French renamed the Bois de Belleau to the Bois de Brigade de Marine.[68] The entire 4th Brigade of Marines received the highest honor from the French government, the Croix de Guerre, for their service at Belleau Wood and Bouresches. From Germany, a translated document, found in the *History of the 96th Company*, detailed the courage of the Marines during the attack on Belleau Wood and Bouresches:

---

65 Harrison Cale, 189-90.

66 Ibid.

67 *History of the 96th Company*, 51.

68 "Wood of the Marine Brigade."

> The 2nd American Division must be considered
> a very good division: even an attack division. The
> different attacks of the two regiments on the Bois-
> de-Belleau were executed with courage and dash.
> The morale effect of our fire could not seriously
> stop the advance of the infantry; the morale of the
> Americans has not yet been sufficiently tried.

The Marines had turned the tide of the war, stopping all hope
Germany had of taking Paris.

Letter to Mother, June 16, 1918

Somewhere in France.

Dear Mother:

I can hardly write you. Living has been too intense the
last three weeks. Before I get a chance to write about one
thing, something else that overshadows it happens. At
present I am in a field hospital for gas. Don't be alarmed,
however, for my case is slight and not dangerous. And
on my body only, for I kept my mask on and saved my
eyes and lungs. We were in it four hours in the heaviest
bombardment I ever saw; they gave us about two gas and
one high explosive, and some sure came close. I didn't
turn into the hospital the first day and tried to stay on
duty, but the sweat brought it out, and we had another
bombardment that night. A three-inch shell exploded
within almost ten feet of the hole where I was lying, and
loads of them came so close you almost thot you were hit.

We went over the top about ten days ago, in a daylight
attack. We advanced three kilometers, the last 50 yards in
a perfect hailstorm of machine gun bullets. Had anyone
told me a person could live in it, I'd have laughed at him,
but twenty-four of us, with one lieutenant, in my platoon,
made the town of Bouresches and cleaned it up and held

it till reinforcements came up. We captured machine guns, ammunition and all sorts of stuff. The boche won't fight tho, close up; they run. They left the town but covered the roads with machine guns which we couldn't take with our few men. They retired that night tho, when our reinforcements arrived.

The town was heavily bombarded all the time we were in it and we repelled a raid on it one night. We are sure on an active front this time and have seen more fighting in a week than we did all the time in the trenches. When we came up first, we were the third line, and inside 24 hours were the first, but we didn't give anyone in rear of us that chance, instead made our drive. We had to dig ourselves in this time and there never was so much digging done so willingly before in the Marine Corps.

Bob was over at our headquarters yesterday just as I was leaving for the hospital, so I got to see him for a minute.[69] He looks older and much more experienced, better looking; has a moustache "Francais" says he's getting along fine. I was sure glad to see him. Send this letter to Lois as I won't get to write her.

Stanley got wounded in action, I understand, not dangerously from all I can hear. A bullet in the shoulder. He is lucky.

Our Brigade has been cited by Pershing a sufficient number of times to wear the French decoration which the Verdun regiments wear. I'll write whenever I can. You don't know how lucky I feel that I am writing at all and still on the top side.

Much love,
Tom.

O. K. Capt. Gamache.

---

69 Bob Hood

Letter to Mother, June 19, 1918

Somewhere in France.

Dear Mother:

I am at an American Base Hospital in southern France, after stopping at three or four others on the way. Everything is fine here and they make you think you are at home in every way. Last night was the first good night's sleep I've had in three weeks, and also we got 'bon' chow here. At the front we slept on the ground, if ever we slept, and got our rations from the packs of the stiffs, as we were on the advance.

We got a chance to see what war is this time, for fair. The road we came up on was simply lined with civilians going to the rear. It is certainly pitiful to see them—mostly old people with all their possessions on wagons, carts, even wheelbarrows, and on their backs; and all tired out with traveling, perhaps a couple of days. It is enough to make a man want to fight. Every one knows the Americans were at Chateau Thierry so there's no harm in saying we were in that action. As I told you we became the front line inside of 24 hours after we took up our position, as the Hun was on a big drive, and the French were hopelessly outnumbered. The first day we witnessed them retire from in front of us on perfect order under heavy shell and machine gun fire, little guessing that in a few days we would advance in a much heavier fire.

When our time came, we did tho—advanced between three and four kilos in daylight in the face of a half dozen Hun observation balloons and without barrage.

Our platoon advanced across an open field whereas the rest of the company had some woods as cover, but we entered a town and cleaned it up, with 24 men and found out to our own satisfaction, that Heine will run every time, and if in a tight place, it's "Kamerad." But it's hard to hear them when they've been cutting you to pieces with machine guns. They had a machine gun company and two battalions in reserve at this town, so you see what fighters they are. They have a splendid machine gun tho, but are poor marksmen.

They shelled our town continually, then so we had little rest, but few casualties. We lost our skipper in this drive and I believe there wasn't a man who wouldn't have gone in his place. He was surely a soldier and a regular fellow. Too careless of his own safety. I was a runner the first night in the town, during the organization, and once ran smack up on a Boche outpost, not knowing just where our lines stopped.

Later we were in reserve in a wood where we were shelled day and night; we all wished for a vest pocket dugout, for every time you moved you must dig yourself one. In the town a one-pounder tore a hole within arm's reach of my post and I thot that a narrow escape, but over in the wood one night a boche .77 exploded not 15 feet from the hole where I was sleeping—not much sleep, I'm not fooling.

In reserve, I helped carry back some wounded from the front lines. The Boche would snipe you even at that, but they are not all like that; some dressed wounds of our men and let them return to our lines. We were up against some of their crack troops, some of the Kronprince's Imperial Guards, so I've decided I can whip the biggest hun in the Imperial army. We haven't been in the line as long as some Americans but our division was the first to put on a drive and hold the ground gained. The Americans don't savvy this retire stuff. We've got plenty of formations for attack but not one for a retreat. The Marines have never been on the run yet and I know darn well the Fritzies can't do it.

We had some hot fighting up there, but I wouldn't have missed it for the world and it's sure given every one in it a lot of confidence in themselves. The only thing we can't beat them at, is the 6-inch stuff and we have to leave that to the artillery, and they are sure doing it. But a fellow can't fight back at a high explosive shell and it's the hardest thing of all to endure continually. A fellow has got to have something to hang on to, or he goes to pieces as some of them do. I am thankful my parents have taught me what that something is to be. When you lie in your little dugout, and shell burst so close during a bombardment that they push you about in it, you wonder what is saving you from a direct hit, and you've simply a Divine Providence to thank for it.

Some of the shell holes are terrific—20 or 30 feet across, and half as deep; of course most are much smaller. The big shells are the easiest to dodge, for you can hear them coming longer. The three-inch or boche .77 mm. is mean, as it comes pretty fast and there are lots of them. We get satisfaction in knowing tho, that the French .75's send over about 5 to 1 to them. The one-pounders are impossible, the whiz-bangs, as we call them; they shoot at such short range that they're on you by the time you hear the report.

Bob Hood came up to see me for a few minutes the day I left the lines for back here. I sure was glad to see him. He's the only fellow I've seen over here that I knew on the outside. He's looking fine and getting along splendidly, he says, and of course they have a better time of it than a doughboy.

Since they have again restricted parcels, don't worry about that stuff I sent the request for. I can get the razor blades, etc. now. And it's no good to have anything more than you wear on your back, for you'll lose it in action, so don't worry, I'll have all I need and more too. It's no telling when we'll get mail, possibly not till we get back to our organization, and keep this same address till I find out differently.

I'll sure take back the unkind things I ever said about France last winter. Since the first of May the weather has been superb and the country itself is simply beautiful, you can't be long in France and not love it. We even see some 'belle madam'selle' here.

I am not in bed and am as well as can be except for my burns which will heal quickly, so have no fears about me. They have my clothes tho so I can't go out much. Anything I've been in tho has done me a world of good and I'm sure in a 'bon sector' now, so rest easy about your Marine in sunny France. Stanley was wounded, not seriously from all reports I could get. I didn't get to see him. Am hoping we'll get back again all, in the 96th some time, and at least the 6th.

We get papers here and it really is a treat to read about how things are going again, instead of knowing only what's happening within hearing distance.

I must close this now. I was going to ask for Lois's address but she'll be gone again before I get a chance to use it. I hope granny is still improving. I'm going to try to write her next.

Much love to everybody,
Tom.

O.K. F. N. Drake
1st Lt. 128 Inf.

CHAPTER FIVE

DIJON

AFTER BEING EVACUATED with severe gas burns, Tom found himself at Base Hospital #17 in Dijon, France on June 19, 1918. In Dijon, most of the Marines that had arrived with gas burns were able to return to duty after about 10 days of treatment. The commandant of the hospital, who Tom says was a Colonel, wanted to see what the long term effect of the gas would be on the men. According to Tom, he "got up the idea that this bunch of Marines would make him guards for the hospital and the hospital grounds there. And I guess he wanted a squad or maybe 2 squads, so he sent orders down and asked if we would stay and do guard duty and be subject to evaluation for the hospital. Well he asked me that, and I thought well, it wasn't an order, he wanted volunteers, so I thought might as well."[70]

Tom and the other Marines that agreed to stay were given tents in the rear of the grounds once they were healed enough to leave the main hospital. They were assigned guard duty for eight hours and given sixteen hours off. This left them with a lot of free time and they were allowed to get passes into the town. To help with mingling in town, Tom began taking French classes from a Red Cross woman. Before the war, she had taught French in New York and come home when the war started and set up a French class for soldiers.[71]

Tom had taken some French in college so his language skills were better than the rest of his class. Through this, he was given an opportunity to get acquainted with a French family. The family consisted of an older gentleman who was a coal merchant,

70 Interview with David Kirk.

71 Tom's Memoir.

his wife, two sons, and his daughter. "He had a son in the French army, and a daughter that was about 18 and engaged to a French soldier."[72] They had Tom out for dinner once in a while and he would see them about twice a week. He took them American cigarettes and chocolate that he could buy from the hospital canteen.

Tom's duty at the hospital was to stand guard at two gates and to act as honor guard for burials. The latter routine was a daily routine with some days requiring several trips to the cemetery as more troops flooded the hospital from the front. Tom mentions that the Chaplain conducted short but impressive ceremonies. Tom continued this duty throughout the remainder of the war. Even after the armistice, he remained in Dijon doing guard duty for the hospital.

Letter to Vera and Everybody, June 24, 1918

Somewhere in France.

Dear Vera and Everybody:

Well, I have more "peace time" experiences to write this time than I did last. Yesterday I had my first liberty in town and tho there was a ball game at the park, I spent it wandering over the town gazing like a yokel. Remember this the first large town in France I've been turned loose in. It has boulevards and parks as pretty well kept and straight as a city at home, but most of the streets are narrow and crooked, so that you can only see a few blocks in any direction.

We set out down the 'main drag' which we found by means of the trolley tracks, and walked. The sidewalks, when there are any, are quite narrow and every one walks indifferently on them or in the street, which is paved with cobble stone. It is quite customary to see a soldat promenading, himself on the walk, and his lady

---

72 Tom's Memoir.

in the street. As it was Dimanche and also most of the soldiers—I mean French ones—on permission, we saw croix de guerres and military decorations without number.

The women are all very well dressed indeed, and it is not hard to understand why the female population of the world copy their style from France. It is also strikingly evident that the men—at least of America—do not. They dress quite differently somehow. Especially the young ones not yet called for service. It is not unusual to see a chap of say 18 in knee breeches and short sox, and some even add gloves and a cane; so sometimes it was hard to keep a straight face.

The streets are broken often with a large circle, in the center of which will be some piece of statuary and parking and perhaps a fountain. Everything is quite clean, in contrast to some of the villages we've been billeted in.

Cafes are frequent and are well patronized. France without 'vin rouge' would be Bryan without grape juice. The champagne is the only thing fit to drink they've got tho. The British Tommie comes in for his beer and the Frogeater for his 'vin rouge' and the American has to have champagne.

The English are sure interesting fellows and I'd like to go to England. You have to listen as close tho, when they talk, as you do to a Frenchman, or you won't understand. They are ultra-Bostonian, I guess you would say, only it's all their own. Some of them will admit tho that some Americans speak good English. A couple are so typical they might have dropped out of a book. I can picture them in London before the war. They have seen some hard fighting, tho, and take it as a matter of course. Can tell some wonderful tales, too, as can some of these French men, who speak English.

I had the rare good luck to talk to a French interpreter, who was an old-timer and he was full of interesting things which probably wouldn't bear repeating in a letter.

The Americans have very little tendency to take prisoners but those they do take say lots more would come over if we weren't so quick on the trigger. They are so dam treacherous tho, you can't ever tell. They'll send out a few and as you go to take them and are a bit off guard, their comrades open up on you with a machine gun. Other times an innocent party of them may try to give up and you shoot them down. But you can see they are sick of it or they wouldn't care to surrender so easily. They'll earn all their American prisoners. Quite a number of them speak English which makes it bad sometimes.

At an evacuation hospital on the way down here, my bunk was only across the aisle from a major's of our regiment. He kept the ward laughing and sure had a good line. Said early one morning while they were lying in a field waiting the time to go over the top, he saw a white rock and decided to sit down and did and next heard "Say, for the Lord's sake, get off my face."

Had a dish of ice cream the other day. First since I left the U.S.A. Had fresh strawberries on it. The "Y" in camp here has it occasionally. They have beaucoup fresh strawberries and cherries around here now.

We went into a restaurant uptown yesterday evening. Before we said a word, he served us wine or beer as we preferred and then beats it and comes back with a big bowl of soup, followed by an omelet, then the meat course of pork chops, and french fried spuds and a dessert of "Fromage swisse" which I had never thot of as dessert before. That, I suppose was the ration for each customer, as they advertised outside "a la carte." Contrary to some reports, we are served bread, tho not in an unlimited quantity. The cheese tho was what got me. All done up in a little paper cylinder about an inch tall and the same in diameter.

We have good American bread here at the hospital and lots of it. It sure tastes good after a long siege of French war bread and Argentina beef.

I'll tell you what we had for dinner today, but not how much, for you'll all be scared you won't be able to feed me when I come back, if I did. Roast beef and gravy, spuds, corn and rice pudding. Also we get sugar and milk here which is quite a treat, even tho the milk in water can cow. We got some Red Cross bags with writing paper, toilet articles, cigarettes, etc., also cards.

Recall to mind, Vera, the name of the main thoroughfare where we went to college, then consult a map of France and you can tell where I am, without greatly exercising your mental capacity.[73]

I must close this now before I incur the undying enmity of the censor. I'm taking for granted tho, that they have a little better facilities than at the front, where I hated to write more than a line or two.

Lots of love to everybody,
Tom.

H. H. L.

Letter to Tom from Granny, July (day unknown), 1918

Dear Tom,

I want to thank you for your fine letters; we are always so anxious about you & so glad you have been protected in many dangers. As you say only a Divine Providence could have protected you & if we trust God all will be

---

73 Tom speaks of Cajon Street to pass to his family, through the censor, that he is Dijon.

well. It is a comfort to you. Know God can protect from
all harm & danger. Read in 91st Psalm & many shall fall at
thy side & ten thousand at thy right hand but it shall not
come nigh thee. The Allies are surely having great victorys
& oh I do hope the war will soon be over. We hope you
have not been in this last terrific fighting. So nice you can
have some enjoyment in the hospital.

Three of your letters are printed in Spearville paper
this week & one in Hutchison news, but Sallie had one
printed in Carlisle papers, so you see how much they are
appreciated. Mr. Gilmore was here a moment ago. He
said they were fine. I do not improve very fast but am so
thankful I am much better than last summer. Can walk
pretty well with a cane. Can't use my hand yet, but it is
improving. Em has told you all the news, so I won't. We
will soon have a manless town here. I am so glad your
folks will soon be back to live in Spearville. I hope it is
all for the best. Bob is with no friend. I do think if I could
only do something things would not seem so dreadful to
me. When I sit alone & think… it all seems terrible. You
away off in France enduring so much, but as you said you
were better for all you had passed thru so I hope I am
stronger for what I have to endure & hope I am patient &
not complaining. We are all so proud of our boy in France.
How proud your Grandfather would be if he were living &
knew what you are doing for humanity. Write often as you
can.

Much love,
Granny

Letter to Folks, July 1, 1918

Somewhere in France.

Dear Folks:

The impossible has happened at last. The Marines got paid yesterday. Every day since Tuesday we were to have been paid, so we had about given up hope and I was on liberty and heard they were paying by the merest chance, but got back up here before he left. Today I have another month's pay coming, as he paid only for one month.

Last night the "Y" had a couple of singers here and they entertained royally. They both had splendid voices and sang things every body knew mostly. As it was the first of its sort I had heard over here I appreciated it immensely. They ended up by every body singing and sang the whole repertoire of soldiers' songs, except possibly a few marching songs that were a trifle passe. Anyhow they sure had an enthusiastic crowd. The Tommies sang a couple of their "Blighty" songs and sure put their heart and soul into it. They usually go to England when they are wounded and they want to so badly.

Yesterday we were out in town and went around to some of the old churches. There is one built in the eleventh century, and others not quite so old, but equally as grand and beautiful.

The work in stone is marvelous and there is so much of it. All the pillars and everything inside and also some on the outside. Large oil paintings on the walls and beautiful art windows in the rarest colors and all of that celebrated glass, the formulae for which has been lost. These churches are beautiful but are not especially celebrated over here, so imagine some of the noted ones, at Rheims and Amiens, etc. that the Hun is destroying.

The older church has the more carved wood and stone and is more ornate in decoration. Has carved wooden

doors and elaborate work on the outside. The newer one
we were in is not so fancy and much more plain. The
pillars and walls are plain white stone alternating with a
stone tinged ever so slightly with a pale rose color.

In this one, on either side of the altar were patriotic
statues which are very pretty, especially the one of Joan
d' Arc. The base and statue is white marble but the base
covered with flowers. A background is formed with fine
flags (3) tricolor and two of her banners.

They have lots of flowers over here and the churches
are full of them and they are arranged with all the artistic
skill so noted in the Frenchmen. At the steps are the poor
always, asking for their sou with a silent appeal, which
completes the scene as you read about it from books.

The newer church is more mixed in architectural plan,
but the older one is true to the one style of its period.

I happen to be on the third floor at the hospital and
from the window in the hall we can see a city on a hill,
surrounded by a wall. It is as old as this one and was once
a very historic place, both in religious and political history.
This town itself was the capital of a province which at
times was as powerful as France itself. So you see we are
on quite historic ground.

One of the "Y" workers who has been here some time
told us a lot about the city. Also the "Y" secretary one day
showed us a lot of kodak pictures he had taken on a trip of
his to Nice and told us all about it. It sure is a wonderful
trip and splendid things to see.

Am reading 'Quo Vadis' in some of my leisure moments.
Don't you think I'm getting a bit heavy.

One of the lads in my company died here the other day.
The funeral is to be this afternoon. Our boys are to be pall
bearers, firing squad, etc. so I will take part in a military
funeral in a land where that is a much too common affair.

There will be an honor guard of Americans possibly
also French, a quaint old-fashioned hearse with the coffin
covered with the Allied colors. The undertaker, an oldish

official, uncomfortable in his long black frock and high wooden hat, painted in a shiny black, sits on his high stool driving a pair of splendid big black horses.

The whole is preceded by the chaplain and perhaps a padre in whose cemetery the body is to be buried, and a detachment of the guard of firing squad.

I read Irv Cobb's story in the Saturday Evening Post about being at the front when the push was on. From what he wrote, I know how much more I saw than he and how much more I was in it, and I'd give a bit to be able to tell it as he is able to.

He tells of a little old woman, waiting at the roadside to be evacuated from a shelled and shattered town, who looks up at him with a smile, and her chin quivers as she smiles.

These things we saw also, as did every one on the road when the Hun was on the advance pushing out the civilians from their homes the second time after they had made their feeble beginning to reclaim their Hun-wasted lands.

I wonder which will be the more indelible on the soldier's mind; the scene of the battle fields he's crossed over, or that endless stream of tired, travel-stained, travel-worn old people, with what of their possessions they were able to salvage, marching on their endless journey to—they know not where, with the smile on their lips as their chin quivered, which only the brilliant writer could find words to describe.

I must close this now. It's nearly time for chow, and you know a Marine never misses that ceremony.

Love,
Tom.

O.K. Oscar T. Slagavol
2nd Lt. 128th Inf.

Letter to Folks, July 5, 1918

Somewhere in France.

Dear Folks:

One more glorious Fourth passed. We celebrated; at least we ate. Had chicken, and it was good, too, believe me, mashed spuds, peas, pumpkin pie, you know my failing, and cake, coffee, and nuts. Also the Red Cross gave cigarettes, oranges and cigars, and in the afternoon, ice cream.

I ventured out into the city after dinner. It was a holiday and every window flew a couple of flags and lots of them five or six allied flags.

There were some shows but we weren't able to go because we're not trusted out after eight o'clock. I'd like to go to a French Theatre once, if only out of curiosity, but not a chance, I guess.

I thot I had seen all of the 57 varieties and many more of French uniform, but alas, yesterday we saw one that beat us for awhile. At last decided it was a naval officer in full dress. He surely would make some high American lodge officials green with envy for he was sure decked out. Even noticeable among French officers, and they sure have splendiferous uniforms.

I came in and sat down beside a little National Army chap, the other night at the "Y" and got to talking to him and found he was from Bucklin and knew a few people I know. Got a little information about Ross's regiment, too, as he was close to them at that camp. Said he thot they would leave soon after he did, so probably they are already in France. Also met a fellow from Hutchinson who knew the Leidighs there, also Burns.

A doughboy from a regiment of regulars, the other day, said to a bunch and I happened to be there, "I'm not a Marine, but I know who did the best fighting up there;

you fellows had it lots hotter than we did." That's pretty good, for ordinarily the regulars sure have it in for the Marines.

Well I must close this now. Don't seem to have anything of interest to write.

Lots of love to all,
Tom.

Letter to Folks, July 8, 1918

Dear Folks:

No news, but I'll write anyway and let you know everything is all O.K. still.

Is quite warm here now and bright sun every day, but cool nights, as always. We sleep under two blankets all the time.

Today we went on a hike. Just a short hike to see what we could stand and how it would affect us. Went far enough out of town up on a hill and could look over the town and the surrounding country. It is sure a pretty sight, and away across from us on the other side are some high bluffs, for this, like most all of the towns, is in a valley.

Last night we had a very interesting talk on Belgium, by a daughter of the Belgian Ambassador to France. She only just left Belgium last September, so has been through lots of the horrors and hardships and speaks from first hand. Her home was in Brussels, which has been perhaps the most fortunate of all the cities.

She didn't tell us much of the atrocities for she said, truly, that every one had read them, and they could believe them or no and whether they be true or no, there is nothing so terrible as the reality which she saw and was a part of. She spoke more of the actual conditions as enforced by the Hun, than his crimes.

Told how one little boy said in his prayer "Give us this day our American bread," and that Belgium would this day have long been starved to death but for the efficient aid and sympathy of America. Soldiers have no communication with their people nor the people with them. Thousands do not know whether their sons, brothers, or fathers are alive or dead; having heard not a word since 1914.

They are a people entirely surrounded by the enemy and governed by it, but still retain such loyalty to their government, that on their fete days the crowds dare to shout "Long live the King, long live Belgium."

Back here in the S.O.S. we learn more of the war than when we are really in it. Through the Tommies we've learned much. They don't ask you to believe the tales of the Hun, in fact said they used not to, till they actually saw them. The Jocks, "the ladies of Hell," Jerry crucifies, or rather, he did; he never takes any alive any more; and in return, the jock takes no prisoners.

There's a boy here who was with the Italian army two years ago. Was in the artillery and said often they had to fire their guns at an enemy who could and did roll boulders down upon them. The Italians now have the advantageous positions, however.

There's a Tommy here who is from Palestine, was up at Gallipoli, in Egypt, Mesopotamia and Palestine. Was sure interesting to talk to. He campaigned in some mighty interesting country. Was with the English when they took Jerusalem.

The famous Second Division paraded in Paris July 4. I only wish I had been with them, or even gotten to see it. Our Captain and second in command each got the D.S.C., the former posthumous of course; the handful of "privates" who got the latter, weren't even given mention.[74]

Well must close this for now. You'll all have to see that the whole family gets to see these letters if they want to hear from me, for I'm just writing to "Headquarters" as the rest kept changing their addresses too much.

Love to everybody,
Tom.

Letter to Folks, July 12, 1918

Dear Folks:

I'm doing M.P. duty here now temporarily till I'm fit for duty at the front again. It had better not be long either. I've got the wanderlust, I guess, the "curse of the Gypsy blood" and I want to be on the go and besides I do believe I'd rather do duty in the front line than hold down a soft job back here. I simply don't like it. Besides I have a little personal account to settle with Jerry now and he'd better look alive.

We had an entertainment here a night or two ago, by a concert company from Paris. They gave us some mighty fine music. Their soloist also gave us some songs in English and we appreciated her rendition.

Our casualties are just appearing in papers over here. We're watching them closely for we don't know a thing about most of our men. I'm going up town this PM and give it the once over again. Will try to see some American papers at the uptown "Y." They usually have some. Another reason I'd like to get to the outfit—I'd like to get a little mail and it looks like we won't get any here.

---

74 Captain Duncan received the Distinguished Service Cross posthumously.

There's a Tommy here that has some "repertoire of songs" as "adopted" by the English army. He's quite good and so are they. There is an American girl that comes to the "Y" some PM's and plays the piano and she's usually about to keep up the reputation of the English Tommies.

Well must close this, for there's no news.

Lots of love,
Tom.

Letter to Doc, July 17, 1918

Dear Doc:

I don't have any idea where you'll be when this reaches you, so I'll mail it home and they can forward.

I haven't had any mail since last May, so seems like my family are wiped off the map. Of course it's not from not writing, I know that, only in not getting it forwarded. I know I've got an armload some where.

Well it's not very exciting here. I got tired doing nothing and so got on the guard here at the hospital, but think I'll try to get away with the first bunch that goes and rejoin the outfit. Can't stand the high living here, I guess; anyway I've got to be moving and the sooner I can go the better I'll like it. Even if it's to have another try at Jerry. He's going to catch small hell this time, for I've a personal account to settle besides, now. Have sure enjoyed being here tho, have talked to fellows from every front, including the East and Russia, tho the Russian wasn't at the front in Russia.

Jerry has started another drive, so I see; by the look of it, I'll not get into this one, but there'll be a lot of fighting this summer yet. This job here wouldn't be bad in winter. You could endure the job for the good bed and grub, but I guess it will be me for the 'trenches.'

Had better close this now. Will try to do better next time.

Love,
Tom.

Letter to Folks, August 3, 1918

AMERICAN RED CROSS
(CROIX-ROUGE AMERICAINE)
Base Hospital No. 17, France

Dear Folks,

Nothing new or nothing interesting to write about but only a note so you may know I'm still coming. The last few days have almost seemed like fall here; it's so uncertain; warm as New Orleans, one day, as an old French man told me the other day—proud to let me know he'd been in America too; and then the next day a rain comes up & chills the atmosphere till you wish you hadn't salvaged your overcoat. Am still attending Madame's French class & wish I had a book—left mine in my sea bag together with a lot of stuff I'd like to have. May be able to bum one off of a kindhearted garde malade!

This is the darndest old town Get upstairs here & see a building you'd like to go & see & when you get up town you can't find it to save your soul.

Have read several pieces in Outlook & other papers of the Marines in action. If you happened to too, you know where I was. I can't know how much of my letters go thru' as I never hear from you or anyone anymore. My only hope is to get back to the company. Must close this.

Love,
Tom

Letter to Doc, August 3, 1918

Dear old Doc:

Your letter received this date and was a welcome oasis in a "mailless" desert, it being nearly ten weeks since I've received one, and it was appreciated to the fullest extent, tho deadly in its brevity; but I realize that a man of your position in the city of your temporary residence, has little time for letters.

No use for you to get excited again simply because the Americans are getting into action. There will be plenty of action for some time and these boys that are over here now can't bag it all. Of course I know you won't wait to be drafted, but that for you is a good ways in the future and you'd better go back to Aggies this fall anyway and keep your eyes open and be sure of what you want to get into. Don't overlook either Aviation and Ambulance, and Jake knows a lot about the infantry; you might talk to him. I wouldn't listen to him of course, but they have none of the advantages and all of the disadvantages of all the other branches in spite of their being the nucleus of them all. And Don't overlook the Navy.

Am having a quiet time here but know not how long it will last. I'm ready to go back 'pronto.' Must close this. If you are still at Uncle John's give them all my love,

Tom.

Letter to Folks, August 7, 1918

Somewhere in France.

Dear Folks:

Well, at last I got some letters so now I'm feeling better. I got one from Viv and also one from Emmie, both written about the latter part of June. Judging from the sound of Emmie's there is some news that has already been transmitted and I had to guess as to the exact facts. Was surely glad to get them tho, and may perhaps get more once they're started.

Viv doesn't seem much more encouraged over Florence than ever: he should revolutionize the town for them.

Em said V. O. and Weldon were at Gettysburg. Is that a draft camp, and if so why were they sent so far? I guess none of them need worry but that they'll see France, at the rate they are sending them across. Does Stanley W. have to go? Who has the Grain Belt now? Suppose Mrs. Pine will be working in the Bank, if Bill goes.

Would like to hear of Bob Hood again. I suppose Lois hears if he is all right always. Don't know how to get on the track of Stanley again. Have tried several ways but guess he doesn't get his mail any better than I do. Saw one of the boys who left here a few weeks ago. I hope I get to see as much of France as he did in that short time.

Make Viv go back to Ag. this fall. He's got a couple of years yet before he need go. Even France is only just calling her men of his age, so he doesn't need to get into a sweat. Has Harry Davis been called yet? I suppose so, and Vee must now be a charming war widow.

Em said Jesse L. was swearing because he had to drill in soft sand. Ha! Ha! Wait till he drills in the soft bottomless mud of France, then he will have due cause.

We had a hard rain last night and of course 'my watch on deck' came right in it, and not having a rain coat, I had to dodge them rather.

That's the deuce of this hospital. They took everything we ever owned before we came here and we won't get anything, I suppose, till we get back to a replacement camp.

Am still going to French class but not parle-ing much yet. They are enlarging the "Y" here to accommodate an increasingly large crowd.

Well, I don't seem to have anything interesting to write
about and better close. Love to everybody,

Tom.

Letter to Folks, August 11, 1918

On Active Service with the American Expeditionary
Force
YMCA
Somewhere in France

Dear Folks:

Still no new thing under the sun here except yesterday,
I got a letter from Stan which I was more than glad to
get. He is in a hospital, not a great ways from here. Was
shot thru the right chest, he says, but missed the lung, so
an operation will not be necessary, he is told. I imagine,
perhaps it may keep him for some time tho.

The 'outfit' is not far from here now, we hear. I'd like to
get with them. Wish there wasn't so much red tape. I'm
sure not needed here.

Stan knew a little about some of the old fellows. My Lt.
for instance, whose luck held and he was finally evacuated
with a bullet in the leg.[75] He certainly had a charmed
life, when I was up there. Expect he'll be up and at them
before long again.

We get no mail and no pay here, so our liberty is no fun,
for everything costs money and emphatically so in France.

The Allies are still giving the Hun his money's worth
and it looks mighty good and I believe they can keep it up
from now on. Sure hope so anyway.

Have enjoyed some good entertainments at the "Y."
Had some girls from N. Y. one night and last night a
French troupe, which had an especially good pianist and

---

75 He refers to Clifton B. Cates.

violinist. Also a couple of singers. A Frenchman could no more sing than talk if he should lose both arms in the war. It's always 'comment ca.'

Well, think I'd better close this now. Sure hope everything is coming O.K. with you folks in every way.

Lots and lots of love to everybody.

Tom.
Base Hospital No. 17 A.E.F.
O.K. Chas. Puautlous
2nd Lt. 12 G.B.

Letter to Folks, August 16, 1918

Somewhere in France.

Dear Folks:

You can imagine my surprise today to get the package from you. I had understood they were 'off' entirely and did not suppose you would send it. Was sure tickled to get it.

The sox are fine ones and the knife is a bird. Managed to get some razor blades after I got here but am glad to have them anyway, for I can use them all right. Everything was all right and came thru fine. They didn't open it this time—at least not the canvas. The candy was dandy—not quite the same as eating it out of the pan but mighty good anyway. The button is nifty. I sewed it right on. I thank you for the needle with it too as much as anything for I've been bumming needle and thread for months. But at that I haven't hurt myself any with all the sewing I do.

I wish I had my kodak. It is in sea bag—location unknown—quite likely "finis" as the froggies say. One of the fellows has one tho, so maybe I can bum it and take some pictures with the films.

The capacity of the hospital has been increased considerably and they are using every available space.

Yesterday we moved out into tents in order to make more room. I like the tents better than the ward and it will save us a long climb as we are on the fourth floor.

I should think I'd get some letters since getting the package. Had one from Viv and also Em. I guess I told you and also heard from Stan.

Have a friend here from New York, who promises to buy me the town when the war is over and we get back.

It has been good and hot here the last few days, but I expect you are having much hotter weather. The nights are always cool though, almost too much so.

If I can raise any francs several of us are going to the theatre next Dimanche. La Tosca was given here yesterday but we didn't know it in time to make a Liberty Drive but may be able to make it Sunday.

Guess I'd better cut this short for now. Will write again soon. Many, many thanks for the package, and much love to everybody.

Tom.

Letter to Dad, August 19, 1918

Somewhere in France.

Dear Dad:

Got a bunch of letters today. First mail from home in nearly three months, and maybe I wasn't glad to get it. All written around the 20th and 25th of June. Had about given up hopes of getting any mail here. Was sure glad to get all the news and hear what you all are doing there.

It is too bad you are having such hot weather; we have you beaten in that way, except on the 'line,' where it's got hell cheated.

The package came thru in good order the other day and I was mighty glad to get it, everything was as you said. Tell

Do the candy was licking good and I'll write her soon. I'll try to write that crippled boy a card anyway. The sox are certainly nice. One pair is too small, but the others O.K.

It is dandy for Vee to be able to go to Funston, tho, I guess it's pretty hot and disagreeable traveling.

Good for Ted. Hope he makes loads of money. Guess he's to be the moneyed one in the family; all the rest of us seem a poor hand at it.

They have lots of tomatoes here, and lettuce and I like that of course. Also can get fresh fruit in town of almost every description.

I don't get the News, Saturday Evening Post, or Outlook, and if you're sending any of them, better stop, or else just put the stamp on so some soldier will get it.

When addressed to me, no one else gets it and I don't either.

It is not so hot here. More like Colorado. Hot in day time and cold at night and no long stretches of extremely hot weather.

[Tom was asked several questions and answers them in this letter.]

No. 1. Was your first engagement at Verdun? About eight kilos south and east of that place.

No. 2. Were you in the fight near Chateau Thierry? Yes, on the immediate left.

No. 3. Are you now near Noyon on the Oise? How near? No, when I wrote, we were near the river mentioned, but not in the lines, in reserve.

No. 4. How near Noyon? Perhaps 75 kilometers.

No. 5. What direction from Noyon? West and a little south.

No. 6. How long does a pair of wool socks last you? I have never worn a pair out. Either lost in action, or as at the gas hospital, all our gassed clothes were taken away from us.

No. 7. Do you wear wool socks in hot weather? Yes.

No. 8. How long do they keep a fellow in the mud knee deep at one time? About an average of ten days. Where it is very muddy, boots are issued. Hip boots usually. At Chateau-Thierry it was open fighting—no trenches. Each man dug himself a hole for protection against shell fire, but rarely were they connected. Often we were in the edge of a woods and communicated among ourselves and the rear, out of sight in the woods. It was very dry—no mud at Chateau Thierry. Only the holes would be too damp to sleep in and it wasn't safe to sleep on the "top side."

No. 9. Do you carry your kodak? No, I wish I did. It is in my sea bag somewhere in France.

No. 10. Do they allow you to send us any films? No, the whole business is taboo. They would be destroyed. If I get any, I'll have to keep them till I again get to a place like this.

I am not having such a ripping good time here, as I have no money, but am learning a little French and enjoying the French people and watching their customs.

Last night was talking to a French Red Cross girl who spoke some English; more than I do of French.

Even at the front we don't have it so hard, so don't be worrying about me. You folks no doubt have lots of things just as hard. It is uncomfortable to have Jerry popping at you continually with 77's and 210's (m.m.), but one gets used to it and only has to make up his mind that none of them has your name on it, and go about your biz.

Of course it's not a picnic to charge thru a field or wood swept with a machine gun, and artillery barrage, but it doesn't last long, and after all, is the greatest game of them all, and the Americans are the best sportsmen.

Once you're in the thick of it, you feel good. What is hard is waiting for the word; say in an open wheat field, under machine gun fire, and you have to lie there and take it. It's a tremendous satisfaction when you get there, when you go over. And if you don't get there, you know you've done your best. To die is only an incident anyway; it's the manner and circumstances that count.

Mother asks about that shrapnel cut of mine. It was nothing. A small piece in the small of my back. If it had been larger and gone in deeper, you folks probably would have had a gold star in your service flag. But, no danger, you know they don't "get" the old timers, and we figure we're as near that as any Americans over here.

Just had to stop for chow. Sure get good chow here. The best any place I've been in the service. I'm getting fat in spite of no breakfasts half the time. Irregular hours, but not hard duty, and lots of times, if I have a night watch, I don't get up for it.

Had a letter today from Rich Mills, who has been over some time and was expecting to go to the front when that was written some time ago.

The "no man's land" experience was an outpost affair, which was necessary to hold to protect our position in the line. The ruins of a town enabled us to live there day and night. The ugly part of it was, if attacked, we most surely would be cut off in the rear and we'd have to cut our way out.

Well, I must close this. Hope I'll have something more interesting to write next time.

Lots of love to everybody,
Tom.

Letter to Vera, August 31, 1918

Somewhere in France

Dear Vera,

Aside from the usual artillery activity there is nothing
to report, that is the communique from the quiet sectors.
I have so little to write about that it just about fits me.
Same thing each day. The last week has not been so hot
and actually cold at night. Sleeping in tents we find two
blankets hardly enough. I was fortunate enough one day
this week to get invited to a French home for an evening.
The girl is considerably older that I, so fear not. She has
been in America and taught French there and at present
has three sister at school in Boston. She came home this
year to be with her mother. As her father is now away in
government service. (not military) She has four brothers
who have been through the whole thing and so far none
have been wounded. One, a cavalryman, was thrown from
his horse and a piece of his skull is torn away, so that he is
no longer in the army, but still in service.

That is quite a remarkable record for the family. The
oldest was a private in '14 and is now 1st Lieutenant. Her
mother speaks no English. I managed to converse with her
and she kindly corrected me when I murdered the French.
We had tea, the first real tea since I left home. It was good,
like we make it. You should see the army tea and seeing it
I know you'd decline it. Even I pass it up and I am almost
immune to punishment in the way of eats and drinks now.
Then we had small cookies such as the peasants make near
the Swiss border, a sort of cross between a cookie and a
doughnut. They are very good.

We have rumors of another pay day coming. If we do
I'm going to take private lessons in French as long as I
have to stay here. I have been lucky enough to get to talk
with several French girls who speak English and they do

speak it beautifully. Usually quite correct grammatically and distinctively accented and pronounced. They like to use the English when they have a chance and it is a treat to talk to them.

The French all say, Ah, Marine, they compris all right. Some don't quite gather our uniform for a French Marine is a sailor. They have no branch corresponding with our Marines. Had a letter from Stanley this week, he says he's getting along fine and I am certainly glad. He has had no mail though, he says, and no pay. I must close, am feeling fine as usual.

Love to everybody
Tom

Letter to Mother, September 3, 1918

Somewhere in France.

Dear Mother:

'Hoop, la! La! I have a 'marraine.'[76] I guess you can find the latter word in a dictionary but the other is French slang, I guess.

I was out to see her last night for the first time. My friend, the French lady, who got her for me, told me she didn't speak a word of English. In fact she speaks less English than I do French, but that makes no difference. When our French and English failed us we used Yiddish—that is our hands.

Sure did have a good time anyway; they are regular folks, even if they do speak French, and they were mighty nice to me. The girl is engaged to a Frenchman—a soldier. She is goodlooking but no beauty, and has lots of good taste.

---

76 French for Godmother.

There's no getting around it, French girls have the class. They all know how to dress, but they ruin their complexions with 'camouflage.' However my marraine does not. Both she and her mother smoke. It is France you know; everybody does. She asked me if I was shocked and I was quite surprised that she knew the word. They were more shocked, I think, when I told them I did not smoke.

The father speaks 'German' but it is forbidden since the war and I know so little of it that I didn't disclose my knowledge. In fact most of the better educated French speak German, rather than English. They are simply adorable when they speak English tho, (the girls I mean). Their accent is very pretty.

I guess you'll have me doped to leave before I bring you home a French wife. Fear not, you know I'm a 'confirmed' and immune against French, English and American. But it is nice to be able to talk to a girl without her thinking you are insulting her.

Altho I had had my dinner, they insisted that I eat with them. They had soup 'nationale,' a vegetable, chicken, then cheese and grapes, and of course 'vin rouge.' Each is a course, soup, then vegetable, then meat etc. I'm not crazy about the French wines, but if I refused they would certainly think me crazy. The champagne is the only real drink over here and for a soldier dead broke, it's plenty far out of reach. They also had a sort of plum conserve pie and café demitasse. And oh, you black French coffee.

I rather got my foot in it in one way. I sang with Mlle., her friend, the other night and they want me to sing—imagine me singing for them. Mlle. Ellen, that is her name, wants the 'American Marseillaise' and has promised to teach me the same in French. I am going to take a kodak over and take some pictures some time.

Had the midnight watch last night, which includes a feed, so had only three dinners in the six hours. Make Viv take French in Agg. He'll be 'jake' if he can 'parley—vous' a little.

I am sending a program of an entertainment last Samedi soir at the theatre. The band was excellent, almost on a par with our own Marine band and that is the highest compliment that can be paid. The male voice was splendid—an American. The girl was French and very fine—not such a wonderful voice, but certainly held her audience in the hollow of her hand. Also the pianist was good, but that does not take so well with a bunch of soldiers, and it was mainly soldiers in the audience both Francois and American.

The theatre itself is quite interesting, three galleries, aside from the main stage. None of the luxuriousness of American theatres. Just benches in the nigger heaven and below many seats have no backs. A small stage, as compared with American theatres.

The other day we had a very elaborate funeral. An officer. Had a French gun caisson and French and American escort.

Saw one of the old boys of the 96th, who gained his commission on the field, the other day also. He is at school now, not a great way from here.

Well, must close this now.

Lots and lots of love,
Tom.

O.K. E. P. Scherdell
2nd Lt.. R.I.

Letter to Helen, September 9, 1918

Somewhere in France.

Dear Helen:

Seems that I haven't written you very often, but every
time I write it is for you too, no matter to whom it is
addressed.

There's nothing very exciting to write about, so I would
have to write most the same things and as you may be
right at home—I don't know your whereabouts much
more than you mine—it would only be repetition.

I am an exceptionally lucky cuss, at least here lately,
for I've sure got a home here; tho the folks do not
speak English. The family consists of: 'the girl'—my
godmother—who is very nice indeed, tho she would never
take a beauty prize; she is goodlooking and has very pretty
eyes. Her name is Ellen. When I told her I had a sister
Helen, she said "la neme que moi."

It is a little difficult, for I speak French so poorly and
it is even harder to understand, but they are so nice and
try so hard to show me a nice time. Ellen is engaged to
a French Lt. Her mother is splendid and has good sense
of humor, which saves our lives. The father is a typical
French business man.

We went to a 'Cirque' one day last week and had some
little cousins along. They had some very good acts; tho
some were mediocre, they say: 'C'est la guerre.'

Yesterday we went all over town trying to go to a
movie, but it being Sunday is quite a holiday, as with
our Catholics at home. It is the big day for the cafes and
amusements.

If it is possible, I'm going to take some pictures when I
go out next time.

The French girl thru whom I met Ellen, is very nice
and her mother is a dear. She speaks English and her

mother not a word. I promised to attend church (hers) but have been on watch at that hour so far. Her uncle is a Presbyterian minister in N. Y. City.

She gave me a little book of the Bible in French, St. John. I read part of it in French, and found it not difficult even without a dictionary. Gave it to a French lady here at the 'Y' for her 'Petite fille.' Had pictures, you know and she saw it and asked to have it when I was 'fini.'

Went to another 'Y' entertainment at the theatre Friday night which was very good. Saturday night went to 'Thais' and it was splendid. 'La Traviata' was Sunday but I couldn't get away.

We got paid yesterday in part, so everything is rosy again, even tho it's been raining continually.

The mail has stopped again, tho of course I know you're writing; if I get in a regular outfit again, I'll get it O.K.

Had better close this now.

Lots and lots of love! Ma soeur.
Tom

Letter to Mother, September 9, 1918

Dear Mother:

Just got your letter today, written July 24 when you had received my first one of June 16. Judging from the tone of your letter, I've missed a good deal of news. You speak of moving to Spearville again and I suppose you are there long since now. Did you sell out at Larned, rent or what? What is dad doing? Should think he'd go into the bank, if Will Pine goes also.

I am sure glad you are back at any rate, for I know you'll be happier there and it will be nice for granny also. I seem to get a letter here and there, so I have to piece in a good bit with the news, but am doping it out all right.

Is Viv at Florence, Larned, home or where? Make him go to Agg this fall again. If he knew all I know he most assuredly would. Right now is the only time in the world to get an education, and he will get a commission at the end, besides, if he works, for he's got the right stuff.

You don't know how lovely the French people are to me in whose home I have gone. It is a little hard, but my French improves slowly and Ellen speaks a little English, tho she can understand scarcely a word. So she talks English to me as much as she can and I talk French to her. The French I had at school helps me enough, so that my pronunciation is not so bad, and I can read it fairly well, but have forgotten my vocabulary. Remember lots of verbs tho and that's the worst part. St and th are most difficult for the French to pronounce; they pronounce Stewart without the first T, but I make them call me Tom and the madame says she's my French mother.

Alors, we got paid yesterday, not in full, but enough, so everything is blue and gold again, at least for awhile.

Tell Dorothy, I've seen the airplanes here, but it's nothing to seeing them on the line, for here they all sport a tri-color circle, and there too often a black cross, which means no good for us in any case whether they pepper machine guns at us or locate us to a diligent Boche artillery man.

Perhaps Vee remembers one day, I met a Phi Delt at Shinneman's office a year or two ago; also a Sigma Phi. Well that Sigma Phi was in my company, & of course I didn't know him, but he said he'd harvested out there once & and then we found we'd met before. Funny I scarcely dreamed of meeting that fellow in France the next time. A small world after all. I've kept a lookout for Colo. friends, but have never run across any yet.

Hope Lois is feeling O.K. again, but guess she's glad to have her tonsils removed. She'd been bothered so much.

Is raining here again. I hope the rainy season hasn't started yet.

Had better close this for now. Please do not publish any more of my letters.

Lots of love,
Tom.

Letter to Mother, September 16, 1918

Dear Mother,

This is some stationery sent me by a perfectly nice girl somewhere in America. No doubt I owed her a letter & will continue to do so, there are so many good excuses for not writing over here.

I got a whole arm load of mail yesterday. Twas all old. I have later letters from you but mail anyway & I was glad to get it. There was a letter from most everyone in the connection I guess. Tell my 'socurs' I'll try & write them each a letter soon. Got Dorto's with the pictures. They are quite good except the one of Bob & her together & the one of Vee. Will be interested to get the letter telling of the news about moving, why, wherefore, etc. If property at Larned rented or sold, etc. Am mighty glad any way. Got a letter from Aunt Minnie also one from Mrs. R. A. Branch, which was quite a surprise. Do you know the lady by the way? Her 'Mari' is in the same Army Corps as I am if not the same division. But I've small chance of ever seeing him. Does Lois still hear regularly from Bob.

Dined last night with my 'marraine' & had a very enjoyable time as well as a fine feed. One of her brothers is home on permission, is a lieutenant & apprendre French slowly so it is a bit dificile and I'm about as talkative as an oyster any way. Made my debut into opera and sang the Star Spangled Banner for them.

No new thing under the sun here to tell you about. It is almost chow time so I guess I'd better desist.

Lots of love to everybody.
Tom

Letter to Lois, September 22, 1918

Somewhere in France.

Dear Lois:

Guess I've neglected you pretty badly. But I hope you'll forgive. There is so little to write about when you can write, and when you can't there's so much.

Am still doing duty behind the lines at the same place, and of course enjoying the rest, but feeling rather guilty for not being fighting for I'm perfectly fit.

Last night was at the Theatre—Carmen and enjoyed it of course, tho in French.

Was out at my godmother's house for dinner the other night. Good Lord, and they say France has been at war four years. I wonder what all we'd have had in peace times. It was some dinner anyway and served in elaborate French style. The menus were very pretty and entirely unintelligible to me. I meant to keep mine and send it home but forgot. Had no less than six kinds of wines and liquor during the meal and the evening. Don't tell mama or she'd be terribly shocked, I fear. It was for the brother who was home on permission and he had in several of his friends, one of whom spoke a little English. Had a good time, and didn't break up until an hour quite 'defendu' for American soldiers so had to run the gauntlet of the M.P.s getting home.

Had the extreme good fortune to be present and to take part in a very pretty funeral service the other day. A

Marine Capt. who, being a Mason, had both military and Masonic honors paid him.

Heard from Stanley also this week. He has finally gotten some mail and is feeling fine, he says. Hopes we can get together but it is rather doubtful.

The folks are springing some of their "stuf" on me always, so how's this one? Detail of Tommies headed for the first line, guide says — 'say, old chap, keep your head low there. There's a chap got it in the heel a bit back.'

It's raining and shining by intervals here today. You can't go out without it rains and if you stay in it shines.

Redeheaven is featured by the "Y" here today. Wonder how old Bill will be taken by the soldiers. Fear his line won't get over, unless he has changed since I hear him.

Suppose you are back at school by now, but I seem to have forgotten if you said you were going back to Springfield or not so guess I'd better send this to headquarters and let them address it.

Must close now.

Lots and lots of love,
Tom

Letter to Mother, September 27, 1918

Somewhere in France.

Dear Mother:

Yesterday got letter from dad, Helen, and Dorto written 8/18 and was glad to hear that you were beginning to be settled again at Spearville.

But sorry to hear that you had hurt your ankle. I hope it wasn't serious and that you are none the worse off for it now and enjoyed a good rest.

Know Helen and Dorothy are long since gone to school and guess you and dad are alone with Ted and Bob and they off at school most of the time. Imagine you are most lost in a nine-room big house again.

Is Viv still at Florence? He certainly ought to go to Aggies since he has to wait the call anyway and it's my idea they won't call them up much before 21 unless absolutely necessary, but rather take them over 31 for awhile.

I don't know whether I wrote you last week or not; when you're not real busy you never get anything done and only when you're terribly so you find time for everything. I wrote Vee but remember now you are not together any more.

Not much news tho. Heard Carmen last week, also a "Y" entertainment at the theatre. Was out to dinner at Ellen's and had a nice time, also was out night before last. Their unhandy habit of having dinner at seven thirty or eight o'clock pretty nearly knocks the evening, for I'm due back at nine thirty and can't get away very dependably in the afternoon on account of special details coming up. Also was over to a tea, I guess you'd call it, the other evening with a number of soldiers at a house where they spoke English.

Dad made a suggestion that I write about a number of things that I'd sure like to but they are quite 'defendu' so won't attempt it as they'd only return the letter.

It is forbidden for letters to the states to be published, and the writer is held responsible even tho they may have been properly censored, so the dear friends at home had better read Cobb and Mary Rinehardt instead of the line I write you.

I read a letter in the Chicago paper by an officer—name depleted—who must have been with our battalion in the Campagne sector. My own Lt. attended Military school in Mo. at one time; he may have written Stan.

I don't remember any questions I hadn't already answered. Saw an old Colorado College man one day last week. First one I've seen. Must close this for now.

Lots of love,
Tom

Letter to Mother, October 4, 1918

Somewhere in France.

Dear Mother:

Nothing exciting but only a word to say I am still at the old job.

Last night was up town to a show — a soiree — so they prefer to call them of the "Y." Mostly music and some pretty good stuff.

One night last week, ran across and American pilot in the French army. He is one of the four American pilots left of the old Lafayette Escradille. Has seen four years war and has been four time wounded and in hospital, not saying several other wounds which he didn't go to the hospital for. He is in a French hospital at the present time and is trying to get permission home, as he hasn't had one since the war began.

We were sitting in a café and this supposed Frenchie says "Say, fellows, have you got a cigarette" and we knew he certainly was no Frenchman, for he spoke American, so we chewed the rag awhile. He sure hates himself, but then imagine with as much experience and all, he has a right to.

If you haven't already, you folks had better read "Hellwood" in the Aug. 31 S.E. Post. Aside from a few inexactitudes it is a mighty straight account, and I'm not fooling, I know. The illustrations tho, were not all taken there and those that were — long after we pushed on. He mentions one Capt. Duncan and Lt. Robertson whom I know quite well. There are a few more interesting facts he didn't tell, all of which contributed to making the name of the wood, but which I too won't write, but will maybe tell you some day. "Belleau Woods" is not 'Hellwood' on the French maps, but 'Marine Brigade Woods' now.

Talked to a French boy who spoke English one day last week. His home is in Nancy and has been there thru it all till this year. Was wounded in bed from an aeroplane bomb. Says every clear night meant a raid for a certainty and some cloudy nights. The town also was in range of the Boche artillery, but you see that's how the French 'carry on.'

Was at the movies the other night and saw an American made picture of the first campaign of 1914—a representation of course; the French are rather easy going and you may not think they hate the boche like the English and even the Americans, but if you'd have been present, you'd have seen how they hate them. There's no describing the sound that came from every one in the house when anything boche was thrown on the screen, from the cleverly dressed brutal Prussian officer to the dirty piggish soldiers of the ranks.

Had better close this now as I have to go on a firing squad for a funeral this afternoon. Yesterday there was one of the prettiest funerals I've ever seen. One of the nurses here at the hospital died from a disease contracted while taking care of her patients. It doesn't seem so bad when the fellows go; even when you lose your pal on the way over the top or in a bombardment, but when American girls go, too—well, that is war.

Hope mama is much better by now and that granny keeps on improving.

Lots of love to everybody; tell the girls I'll write soon.

Lots of love,
Tom

U.S.M.C. A.P.O. 721 A.E.F.

Letter to Mother, October 14, 1918

Somewhere in France.

Dear Mother:

Got a bunch of mail again yesterday. Some of it as late as Sept., so think I'd better get busy and do some writing. Got yours of August 27 also one from Lois, Helen, and Emmie, Vee. Lois gave me Zeno's address. He isn't exactly at Dijon I see, but may be able to see him anyway. Had a nice letter from Aunt Annie at San Diego too; guess she has had quite a time of it. Says she is much better there now.

Well, judging from the news we have here, Viv will never be called, and not much use to enlist, as I guess they'll soon be sending men back instead of across. I can scarcely believe it. Guess no change for the armies tho, till Germany has come thru with everything she promises, for her word is no good.

I guess Pershing was right, theoretically at least, when he said "Heaven, Hell, or Hoboken by Xmas."

Had a real nice long letter from dad a while back and haven't got it answered yet, but will soon. Told me about the affairs at Larned, etc. which I was interested to learn.

There's not much to write about and the French mademoiselle has started her French class so I'd better stop writing.

Lots of love,
Tom

Letter to Folks, October 22, 1918

Somewhere in France.

Dear Folks:

I am enclosing said much heralded Christmas coupon. I guess the best address will be the old Company address and it will reach me no matter where I might be.

As to what it might contain — I can't think of any needs and it's no use to send anything else for it would be lost no doubt — not in transit but by me later, as you can never be sure of having anything very long and it's best not to have much.

Put in a couple of Kolynos toothpaste and a good brush; a pair of ordinary light cotton sox, a couple of rolls of Vest pocket films. The rest with cake, candy or both. Don't worry about my getting sox or woolen goods, as we get all we need.

It has been raining all day. Tonight we have a fire in our little wood stove here in the tent, and we are as dry as can be, and almost too warm. Entirely too much so according to the French standard. They don't have much fire. If it were not so wet, it wouldn't be so cold, as it is, it goes thru you. Yet you see every day the French kids going to school with little short sox,

Their bare little legs almost blue, but they are used to it I guess and don't mind.

This pen is so abominable that I'll have to quit.

Lots of love,
Tom

O.K. A. B. Pitts
1st Lt. A.S. U.S.A.

Letter to Dorto, October 27, 1918

Dear Old Dorto,

Seems an age since I've written you so I hope you're very forgiving and aren't terribly mad with me. I'm terribly neglectful I guess. When you are the busiest is sure the time when you have time for everything. There's nothing very rich, rare or racy to write about so you have to read a dry old letter at that after all this waiting. Was down town in the Museum of the Fine Arts the other day. It is surpassed only by the one in Rome & in Paris now since the Hun has pillaged notable galleries in Belgium. It is a very interesting trip, only wished I could have more time. It is not open to the public so had to go thru' with a party & of course rather hurried. It is in the palace of the Dukes of Burgundy built in the 14th century, a very interesting & beautiful building its self. Aside from all the sculpture & paintings, they have some rare old furniture, jewelry, weapons, etc. of the Duke's, and the most notable of all are a couple of Tombs of the Dukes' which are marvelous, & have work which took years & years to do.

Not much doing here. Had a letter from Stan not so long ago. He is fine he says. Have had mail written the first of Sept. now. Did Viv go back to school this fall? You'd better not get too intelligent in French or you'll be correcting me all the time when I come back & tell me I speak slang. Think I'll go out & see my French girl to-night & see how much I've forgotten.

Well, I guess I had better ring off now, Dorothy.

Lots of love to Lucy & Clyde, & yourself.
Tom

T. L. Stewart, U.S.M.C.
A.P.O. 721, A.E.F.

Letter to Mother, November 2, 1918

Somewhere in France

Dear Mother:

Guess I missed writing last week, but not much difference for there's not much to write or write about. We are having 'mauvais temp' again and of course enjoying to the fullest extent of a foreigner.

I kid the Frenchmen I know by saying 'La Belle France' on days like this.

Took a couple of short trips around here this week. Am going to try to get up to see Zeno this week.

Had a letter from Stan this week. He is now on the coast and having a good time and not too hard duty and with lots of the old fellows.

He saw Deb Teed over here. Used to go to school with him, you know.

Have not had any mail for some time so am about due I think for a little, but expect nothing any more and then am not disappointed.

Well I guess I had better quit. There is such a mob here, a fellow can't attempt to write.

Lots of love,
Tom

Letter to Tom from Granny, November 4, 1918

Dear Tom,

I was so glad for your letter which came yesterday. Of course I have heard from you as the folks have had letters frequently. I sure am happy that the folks have come back to Sp. & are settled again in their old home. Your mother seems happy—don't know how your Dad feels about it, but he surely looks much better, has gained 10 lbs. since he is here & that is worth so much. His voice too is better. He has been fixing up around the house & lawn. Everything was so out of shape and has done many little jobs for us so he is always busy. I suppose you have heard of the terrible epidemic of influenza that has stricken this country since Sept., so many deaths in camps & large cities. We have some cases here in town now & one death last week, a young Hepplehaus. Also heard last week that John Reidel died in France. These surely are anxious days, but at this time the victories overseas is very encouraging & we do hope the war will soon end & our dear brave boys will soon be home. We are truly thankful God has been with you and protected you from the many dangers you have passed, tho how sad your cousin Paul Irwin lost his life & so many other brave noble boys.[77] How many sad homes, but all for a great cause & we must all make sacrifices. Helen was home three weeks. All schools closed on account of influenza. I do miss her so much, was so much comfort for me when others are busy. I am so well and time seems long when I cannot do anything except read & write some. My eyes give out when I do that too long. I do try to be patient, but it takes a lot of courage sometimes to be still & wait. I do gain but very slowly but am so thankful for that. Can walk easier but can't use my hand. There is so much to be done in this busy world. I would like to help.

I wonder if you have not yet heard of Will Pine's death. I sent you clipping from paper. I see our Kansas boys have been in another Hell fight something like Chateau Thierry. Uncle Ed's boys were in that of the 29 of Sept have not heard from this yet. Mrs. Ward sent us a letter from Stanley and we all enjoyed. Told of sensation when wounded, also of your bravery. Hope you hear from him

---

77 Paul Irwin, Tom's cousin, was killed on September 26, 1918 by an artillery shell while going over the top at Vauquois, France.

sometimes. Glad you enjoy the French girl. Must be interest long to see all the family.

With lots of love from,
Grannie

Letter to Bob, November 5, 1918

Dear Bob,

I guess you will have celebrated your birthday long before this reaches you but I'll write a line to you any way. I suppose you are quite old and dignified by now, especially the dignified. Are you still glad that you have moved. And how do you like the 'small town' kids after life in the big city. Doc's your teacher stay there also, if so you ought to know him real well by now.

I was out to see my marraine last night but she was sick. Spanish 'flu.' So I parlay-ed with her brother and her mother. Her older brother that was here so long is in the aviation now and this one goes soon to Siberia so they are leading a gay life.

I haven't anything very interesting to write, doing the same old thing every day and not much for excitement and the paymaster has disarmed us I guess.

Well, I don't seem to have much news so had better cut this short.

Lots of love to everybody and all kinds of best birthday wishes for you.

Tom

T. L. Stewart, U. S. M. C.
A. P. O. 721 Am. E. F.

CHAPTER SIX
ARMISTICE

ON NOVEMBER 11, 1917 at 11:00 AM, the armistice went into effect. The war was finally over. After four years of fighting, the world was finally able to rest. For the United States, the last five months inflicted severe casualties. Out of an estimated 365,489 casualties, approximately 53,000 were killed in action, 54,574 died of disease or other natural causes, and approximately 260,000 were wounded.[78] Tom's 96th Company suffered casualties of 123 killed and 491 wounded during their time in the war.[79] After the signing of the armistice, the 2nd Division was tasked enter into Germany as part of the Occupation Force. However, Tom remained in Dijon on Military Police duty.

Tom continued his same routine of attending French classes, exploring the town, and spending time with his adopted French family. In December, while sleeping late in his tent, Tom was awakened suddenly by Deke Ward. After not being accepted into the Marine Corps with Tom and Stanley, he joined the Army Tank Corps. His tank company was stationed 40 miles north of Dijon. So, Deke told his commanding officer that his brother was in the hospital and he requested to spend Christmas with him.

---

78 U.S. War Department, *The War With Germany: A Statistical Summary* (Washington D.C.: US GPO, May 1919), 117.

79 *History of the 96th Company,* 65.

Deke Ward's Travel Pass Request, December 24, 1918.

Co. B, 302nd Bn., Tank Corps, U.S.A.
A.P.O. 714 Am. Ex. Forces, France.
December 24, 1918

From: Private Vernon O. Ward. #3082511.
To: Commanding Officer, Co. B, 302nd Bn., Tank Corps.
Subject: Request for Pass

Request permission to be absent from camp from 6:00 PM December 24, 1918 to 6:00 PM December 26, 1918, to visit Dijon, France.

My reason for requesting this pass is that my brother is in the hospital in Dijon and I would like to spend Christmas with him.

Vernon O. Ward

Co. B, 302nd Bn. Tank Corps, U.S.A. A.P.O. 714 AEF, France.
December 24, 1918. To: Commanding Officer, 302nd Bn. T.C. USA.

Forwarded approval recommended.

Roy T. Deal
1st Lieut. Tank Corps, U.S.A.

The two had a good visit, an occasion they deemed worthy of opening a bottle of champagne. They spent their meager funds to have a great time in town before Deke had to return to his unit. Shortly after this, Tom was finally transferred out of Dijon.

Letter to Tom from Dad, November 17, 1918

Spearville

Dear Tom:

Well the best news we have & that in which we are particularly reveling now is "The war is over." That is we think so far when this 31 days Armistice is over Germany cannot come back & the old Kaiser slink away & hid like a skunk or sheep-dog. (No man about him) which was no news to us as we all knew he was not a man. Not even a brute. Not even a Demon for he has out demoned his Satanic Majesty.

Well we celebrated for 2 days. Didn't burn up any good fuel or destroy anything useful for we have learned conservation in the last year or two but we did make some noise & sing some & rang the bells & blew the whistles & as the trains went through they blew their whistles all the way through town. Well the same day Tuesday Viv finally was admitted into the Student Army training camp at Colorado College. It is 5 or 6 weeks since he gave up his job & applied for admission. He has had about as hard a time getting in as Vernon Ward had & now I hope they will & I presume they will continue the boys at College training through the year anyhow, as most of them have given up jobs to go.

Well I suppose you & the other boys are about ready to come home now & especially if you walk as you spoke of doing when you went over. Do you want us to send you your skates so you can make better time on the ice? You could go to Norway or Spitybergen & skate across by way of the north pole. Well we are as anxious to have you come home as anybody could be. But since you have gone through the difficult & dangerous part of it, it would be nice if they would send the Marines around a little to the different cities to see how the natives are getting along establishing their new forms of self-government & show them a few things & help them write a constitution & establish themselves substantially & equitably i.e. Give you a taste of the bright side of the life of the Marines as well as the rough side of it which you have already seen. I don't know if we told you Miss Patchen was elected. But she was & 2 other Democrats in this County the other 2 had no opposition & Pawnee County even went Republican this year by from 100 to 400 majorities. Old Democratic County. And Henry Allen is our new governor & Arthur Copper our new senator & Mr. Tincher of Medicine Lodge our new congressman. (Janett Shouse defeated) Some Republicans are going to "Help Wilson win the war."

The "Flu" is pretty bad yet but our schools begin again tomorrow after 5 weeks of "Flu" vacation. No other public gatherings yet. (Our celebration was all out doors).

Vera is home today. Harry D. still at Funston.

This is a sure enough windy day & hazy. Looks just like it did the day of the Omaha cyclone.

The folks are fixing up your Christmas box to send tomorrow. Will write you about what is in it & who gave the different articles. I hope you will get a lot of good out of the camera etc. As I suppose the censor will be off by Dec. 12th anyhow. So you can take pictures & send them also & write what you want to. As I understand that even now the censorship has been lifted from the Associated Press. Anyhow I notice T. R. says what he pleases in the K. C. Star. Well I'll stop now & save room in this letter for the rest of the folks letters.

Lots of love
Your "Dad"

And there is no one we will be as glad to welcome home as Tom.

Letter to Tom from Mama, November 17, 1918

Sunday

Dear Tom:

Of course we have been all rejoicing and celebrating over peace. Although we could hardly believe it at first. The town tried to sing songs on the Bank corner but were such a few men couldn't make much noise. Then we all got in cars and rode around town singing & yelling. Poor Mrs. Pine stood there smiling with tears on her face while they sang "When the boys come home." Every one asks will Tom be home for Christmas. That would be almost too good to expect. We got your label this week, also the little smilage books. Em send you and another letter. Vera had the Kodak for you. She wrote she would bring it up Sat. eve. So she came. The wind has blown a gale almost as bad as the day of the Omaha cyclone only not dusty as that was, but is going down some now. The Kodak is bought with money Aunt Minnie sent for you. The wool socks are the ones Aunt Flo had knit for Paul. The jam jars are from Alma and Lucy. And the watch is from Cousin Anna and I guess the tooth things are from Lois. Helen had knit socks for you but can't get any more in the box. Em & Bob made the peanut candy. Wish we could put more in it. The pictures are from "Po" and Frederick. And we have at last heard from Viv that he got into The Student Army at Colorado College just as the news of signing of the armistice carne. He says he feels like a fool getting at last minute but he tried hard enough. The men who were to go to camps last week were mostly stopped before they started. A few got there but were sent home.

Two week ago when Phyllis Renfrew & Gertrude Westmacott were going back to work, they were talking about you and Stanley. A soldier sat in front of them and heard your name. After Gert got off at Great Bend,

he turned and asked Phyl if they had been speaking
of Tom Stewart and Stanley Williams. He said he was
Private Alexander who knew you at Paris Island. Tom
Westmacott told this from Phyl's letter and thought he
said he belonged to the 88th but I thought you were 82
down there. Anyway, he knew you boys and he was sent
to South America. Helen writes that her Superintendent
has the influenza. I fear he has exposed the rest of the
teachers, but I hope they all keep well. Louise Zeigler
and her mother have both had it. They are expecting to
open the schools here tomorrow after five weeks closing.
But some folks think they ought not to open yet. The
state closing order was lifted two week ago but it was
just getting started here then. Rev. Gilmore family are
quarantined now, some of the children have it. The people
are so depressed with this epidemic that they couldn't get
so excited about peace as they would otherwise.

Dad had a letter from Mr. Roger H. Motten of Colorado
College a week or more ago about you; had heard you
were in France. Wanted your picture in uniform etc. I had
gotten a few more of those with the hat on so we sent him
one and referred him to the article in S. E. Post of Aug.
31 and told him you had been gassed. Suppose they are
trying to make a record. We sent the letter to Viv and told
him to see him if he could. Then "Po" wrote Mr. Motten
about Viv so thought he might see him.

Vernon has a short letter in the News this week or
rather Mrs. Ward sent it. From everything they write they
must have had a stormy voyage. Granny had letter from
Uncle Ed. One of his boys was wounded twice in Sept still
in hospital. Mrs. Stinson is preparing to have Glen home
to celebrate Christmas. Well Tom, if you come I guess we
can celebrate all right whether we have much to eat or
not. We can buy sugar and white flour now unrestricted
however I hope you can get the money we sent you last

week from Ellen and Aunt Annie. Betty Westmacott had at last been sent to the front in France the last letter they had. So guess she will be satisfied to come home now when the time comes. But amid our rejoicing I think of the sad ones who will miss their boys the more when the others come home.

With love,
Mama

Letter to Folks, November 27, 1918

Somewhere in France.

Dear Folks:

Well, I guess it's about time I issue another bulletin to let you know I'm still coming. There's no news, so I can hardly call it a letter.

Has been raining this PM so tonight we have a fire in the tent and are quite comfortable. It is not quite so cold, now it is raining again; we had a stretch of clear weather tho. Our dog is in here chewing on a 'turkey head' so we know we are to have a real Thanksgiving Day dinner tomorrow, and all you Hooverized people in the states can envy us.

Was out at Ellen's last night to dinner. They surely do put out the feeds all right and you'd never believe there had been four years war and nearly as many of food restriction; and of course wines etc. and the et cetera is strong as hell, therefore Tommy lays off of it pretty muchly even tho you nearly insult them to do it. They can't understand such a thing as a 'prohibition state' and to tell them it's 'sans cigarette' also, they know I was lying to them, so I never attempt any explanation.

This afternoon was out to a historic place, "The Well of Moses," which is quite interesting from an artistic standpoint not being able to 'compris' all that stuff, we enjoyed seeing it anyway with a mademoiselle, who was quite willing to tell us all the history of it, the chapel and jardin, but in French of which we partook little.

One day last week we were out to a small ville near here and saw the chateau which was once Napolean's headquarters; there is a statue erected to him in the park surrounding.

Sunday was a bit fete day out at the aviation field; everybody was there. There were planes of all sorts, types, and nationalities, not all of which flew of course but only exhibited.

Of those that flew there was a large Macroni bombing machine which carried about six men and a capacity for a large number of bombs; is driven by three huge engines and is operated by Italians of course. Also a French one of the same type. Several smaller scout biplanes—French—a whole squadron of Americans in Liberty motor, driven planes of the scout type. Then a few small French chaser or battle planes which cut up and put on the stunts everything. Flew at the rate of a 100 miles an hour and over, about ten feet over the heads of the crowd, loop the loop, nose dive, and everything in fact.

Met some American ladies the other day, whose French husbands were in the war. One, a countess, it happens is a widow; her husband was killed with the Americans on a voluntary mission into 'Bochie.' He also was the officer who led the first American raid a year ago.

Is the Spanish 'flu' bad there? I've no word from you and I know it is pretty bad in the states at some places.

The lid is off the censorship now they say. I've already told you I guess most everything that I could in a letter, so I'll not bring up an old story. I might have headed this letter, Dijon, France, tho. That is better than somewhere, I suppose, if not as romantic. I understand the 'outfit' is in

Luxemburg. Haven't heard from Stanley but have a hunch he has gone to the states as he was already on the coast.

Tell Vee when you write her that one of my little Frenchmen sent her a Xmas card the other day. He is a chap about Ted's age, and wanted to send my sister a card, so Harry needn't be jealous.

I really don't know, but it's my guess that you may receive this about Xmas time. In that case I'll send my greetings, as that's all I'm in a position to send and I hope for you all the very best Xmas imaginable, and the happiest of New Years; and I know it will be the happiest of holidays in many a long year for "It's over now" and that's about all that mattered, that it is over and over right.

I know nobody will be quite so happy as the French, for they have endured so much. Theirs has been the burden from the start; their allies have been suffering with them by fits and starts, now this one, now that, but always the French have been in it and really 'carried on.'

Tell all the folks there — The Westmacotts, Lynches, etc. a Merry Xmas for me. Also Mrs. Patchen and the kiddies.

Must close this now with lots and lots of love to everybody.

Tom.

Letter to Mother, December 3, 1918

Dear Mother,

Not much news but that I'm still on the top side and standing to as always — still surviving French weather as well as everything else.

Since the lid is off the censorship, I might be able to tell you some interesting things about conditions, which will no longer aid the enemy, tho I guess it's not really news to you for most everything is published in spite of our strict erstwhile censorship.

The French have no sugar, no oil or gasoline, matches, tobacco, or cigarettes; very little chocolate or coffee; of course the gov't. has some of these and the soldiers get an issue. Bread is still on ticket and without them you cannot buy bread. No candy or sweets of course, and the kids all play the Americans for it. Every kid knows 'good bye' and usually adds 'cigarette?' 'give me gum' or something of that sort. They are all after tobacco or cigarettes and sweets. Gum is a new one on them, for they don't have it in France. Even the grown folks don't know what it is, if you happen to be the first one to have given them any.

Women quite often are on both ends of the street cars, and ambulance drivers are mostly all women; bicycles are very numerous and very few civilian motor cars are in evidence, tho more this last month.

Had a letter from Stan the other day and another today—today's an old one tho. The other one stated he was leaving for God's Country, the 20th of Nov. so no doubt he is enjoying all the blessings of the U.S.A. again and is well on the way to donning 'mufties' again.

I am in a study as to what address to give you. Makes little difference, I guess, so keep on as before. I don't know if I could give a better, but we're missing connections somewhere.

Had better close this for now.

Lots of love,
Tom

T. L. Stewart, U. S. Marines
Okay
Lt. Z. Gass 1st Lt., Ord.

Letter to Folks, December 9, 1918

Dear Folks:

Well, what would knock a fellow colder than to be awakened in the morning by no less than old Deke Ward, who as far as I knew, was still in the states. He tells me he has been across four months and knowing that I had been here, took a chance on finding me and came down. Well he's the same old kid and we sure had a good time from about all points of the compass.

Got a lot of news from home and all, of course and scandal, too. You see I personally have not had any mail for some time, except a couple of letters from Stan. I guess he is in the states by now. I hope so. Ward didn't know that however.

He has lost all his Spearville gang too, it seems but is getting along fine, but working hard. He looks well and has put on flesh since I saw him. He said the same of me, but I'm not as heavy as I was.

Of course he couldn't stay long, so we had to be swift and he didn't see much of the town, but guess didn't care to, tho he said it was the only town he'd been in so far. They came thru England as you know, I suppose, so he has seen quite a bit of country anyway.

Now then there is a matter I want to bring up and I mean it. I asked you not to publish my letters and I thot I was nice about it, but if I must get 'hard' I can, and I don't want any of my stuff in print—compris? I'm writing you lots of things I'd never put in if I were writing for the editor of the 'home town paper' which you should appreciate, it seems to me. Circulate them all you want to but after that—finish. I used to laugh at a lot of stuff they publish and I know mine is no better, and I don't want them laughing at mine. I'm writing for your benefit and not for the general public. You know there are always post

cards or the Red Cross Bureau I can resort to. Now this is
the second edition of this letter. I was afraid to mail the
first, so don't let it happen again.

I can't write much this evening and I go on watch pretty
soon anyway, so I guess I may as well bring this to a close.

I hope every one is well and from all Ward says they are.
He says he hears from Emma regularly, so I am satisfied
on that point anyway.

Lots of love,
Tom

T. L. Stewart
6th Marines, A.E.F.
A.P.O. 721 Base 17

Letter to Mother, December 16, 1918

AMERICAN RED CROSS
ON ACTIVE SERVICE WITH THE AMERICAN
EXPEDITIONARY FORCE
T. L. Stewart
6th Marines
A.P.O. 721, A.E.F.

Dear Mother,

Am fine & all to the good. No news at all to write.
Expected to leave here this week, but delayed again. Will
not be long now. Will probably go up into Allemagne. I
hope so, tho' of course would like to come home but not
in too big a hurry. Received check to-day from Paris &
many thanks. Was not entirely broke yet but appreciate it
just the same.

Hope you are all well & wish for the whole family the
merriest of Xmases & a Happy New Year.

Love,
Tom

Letter to Doc, December 16, 1918

Dear Doc:

Well, I wonder what in the world you are doing and where you are. I am absolutely uninformed as to news of the Stewarts in America.

Had a Xmas card the other day from a friend in Washington D.C. the first U. S. stamp I'd seen in over two months. Had mail from Stan however. He is in the states now I judge; possibly at home.

Old Deke Ward made a flying trip down to see me about a week ago. He has been hearing from Em, so knew a little and I got most of the scandal from him also. He had of course not been away so long so knew a lot of stuff first hand about the old burg.

We both happened to have plenty of francs so put on a good celebration for the occasion, and it's one day we won't forget in France.

Expected to get out of this town this week but orders changed again so we have no idea when; but soon and it can't be too soon for me.

Are you married? The latest reports I had on you, it was expected at any moment. I've cut out writing to all the girls I ever knew for two of them with whom I was keeping a healthy correspondence have gotten married since I'm over here and I think the rest are contemplating it.

I had a check today from a Paris banking house and of course it was duly appreciated. Convey my deepest thanks to whoever started it on its way.

Will have to close this now. Hoping to see you all in a year or two anyway.

Love,
Tom
A.P.O. 721

Letter to Helen from Tom's Mother (written on the back of Tom's December 9, 1918 letter) January 2, 1919

Dear Helen,

Should have written sooner. Was so glad to get Vera home. But was rather scarely about it. Got rather windy before we got here and took a while to get her into a buggy. She couldn't step so high, but it has been so cold since. We couldn't have come for so long and the teachers are coming. Two came yesterday eve.

They sure had a good time seeing Stanley Williams. I went down to see him Sunday evening. As he went through Larned on No. 8. Harry left on that and Althea & Mr. Cuningham went down to go back with me. It was midnight when train got there. I guess they thought I was crazy. But I couldn't let him go by. Of course could only talk a minute. Saw his decorations. He says Tom has them also. The highest honor given by French Gov.

The table runner is sure a beauty. Hope you are well. I feel fine. Too bad Tom thinks we kept on printing his letters. Send this to Viv or Lois or back home or "Do."

Letter to Mother, January 5, 1919

With the A.E.F.

Dear Mother:

Was quite surprised the other day to get a little mail. It was a complete synopsis in itself, for one letter from Vera, written in June, and another, the latest, in Dec. the 6th and the rest spread out in between. I was mighty glad to get it as it is the first since last Oct. The one letter contained the memorial of Will Pine and Bob's picture. Tell Bob I will surely do as she suggests and write her a letter soon.

It is certainly too bad about Will Pine and hard on Mrs. Pine. What is she doing? I suppose Kaiser is home by now or soon will be, with the regulation Y.M.C.A. man's bag of souvenirs.

I got up earlier today than I have for many a Sunday, to meet a Frenchman whom I met at Ellen's who wants to show me a good time, but he also has an ax to grind.

I am still at Dijon, but expect to leave the first of the week either Mon. or Tues. where we do not know, but I will write you from there and will not have to use so much camouflage as formerly to let you know where I am.

I hope dad is working with Harry.[80] How is the weather and also the crops there this fall? I guess they pretty nearly have to be good after the last two years.

HEE! Haw! Em says Jesse loathes the 'belle France.' I seem to be about the only one who has an abnormal love for the country. There are certainly many drawbacks but also many things to make up for them in some ways.

Well mother I think I had better cease this raving 'parce que il faut que je pund mon bain avant mide'.[81] Ask Vera or Em. They ought to be pretty good 'frogs.'

Oh, did I tell you Ward and I had snails the other day for dinner. I swore I wouldn't leave France till I had eaten some. Sure should have been along. They're great.

Lots of love,
Tom

P. S. Oh, yes, was made a corporal at Chateau Thierry, but have no papers, so don't claim it. It's no distinction.

T.

---

80 Harry Leidigh, Tom's uncle.

81 "Because I have to take my bath."

CHAPTER SEVEN
THE AMERICAN UNIVERSITY

TOM REMAINED AT DIJON until being transferred on January 7, 1919 to St. Aignan. He and the other Marines sent to this classification and re-outfitting camps affectionately referred to it as "St. Agony" because of the chaos and poor conditions. Tom also called it the "mad house, mud hole, or anything of that sort that would be most appropriate." There were about 30,000 men at the camp, all awaiting reassignment. This, paired with France's notorious amount of rain, created a large mud hole.

Tom had to put up "quite an argument" to be transferred out of Dijon. He mentions that everyone that remained at the hospital thought he was a fool for leaving. But, Tom wanted to return to his old unit and hoped he would be sent back if he went to St. Aignan. However, after almost a month, Tom was transferred with a detachment of Marines to Camp Rochambeau outside of Tours, France on February 5. Here, the Marines performed guard duty and awaited their time to return home.

While waiting, the American soldiers were allowed to put in to study at Universities around Europe. One of Tom's friends tried to convince him to put in for the Sorbonne in Paris. Tom did not think he would get it so he passed on the opportunity while his friend did apply and got accepted. Seeing this, Tom put in for the American University at Beaune, France and was accepted and transferred to the University on March 24.

The American University at Beaune was established by the National War Work Council of the Y.M.C.A. to allow men who had done initial college work the opportunity to study further.

The University had been placed in Beaune because the Red Cross had erected hospital buildings during the war and they were no longer being used. Other buildings in the area, such as large canvas hangars were requisitioned for assembly rooms and machine shops. The army then erected barracks to house the attending troops and teaching staff.[82]

The University opened its doors on March 17, with thirteen departments: the Colleges of Agriculture, Letters, Fine and Applied Arts, Education, Journalism, Correspondence, Music, Engineering, Business Administration, Law, Medicine, Science, and Citizenship. By April, the University boasted 6,000 students and 600 teachers.[83]

While at the University, Tom traveled across France taking photos along the way. On one trip, he wanted to visit Paris but no passes were being granted for it. So, a friend of his told him to get a pass to Dijon and remain on the train until it arrived at Paris. Tom recalled that he "got into Paris at eight AM and the guard there stamped my pass for 24 hours. I looked for my friend that went to Sorbonne and he showed me around Paris. I went to Versailles and saw the palace." This trip was possible because in moving out of one unit to another barracks his name was omitted from the roll so he was not A.W.O.L.

Tom attended classes until they closed on June 7, even though the end of the term was June 10. The University planned to have more terms but, as soldiers returned home, the student body dwindled until there were not enough around to make the University worth the cost to the Army Educational Commission of the Y.M.C.A.[84]

---

82 Oscar M. Voorhees, "The American Expeditionary Forces University at Beaune: An American University in France," *The Phi Beta Kappa Key* 3, no. 12 (May, 1919): 581-82.

83 Ibid, 582.

84 Ibid, 582.

Letter to Mother, January 13, 1919

On Active Service With the American
Expeditionary Force

Dear Mother,

Well I've made the said long-expected move and am
now in a classification camp at St. Aignon near Tours; am
all equipped & ready to shove off again; let us hope back
to the outfit.

There are nearly 30 thousand men here & all coming &
going all the time, so it is really the mad house that they
call it. It is also a sea of mud & it rains continually, but
that is France so to be expected. Have run across some of
the boys out of the old bunch, on their way back as I am,
will write again & let you know whether we finally land in
Allemagne or elsewhere.

I wish sometime you would write Madame Chapuis,
she certainly has been a very lovely 'French mother' to
me and I can never thank her & Ellen enough. They have
done simply everything for me as if I belonged to them &
insist if I ever want anything to let them know as 'America
is too far.' Also want me to get a 'permissione' for Ellen's
wedding this spring, which I shall if possible.

Madame A. Chapuis
2 Quai Nicholas Rollin
(Cote d'or)
Dijon, France

May write in English as one of the family translates.

Had to put up rather an argument to get away from
Dijon at last. This army is sure funny.

It is not very cold here, only rain, rain all the time & I
really would prefer the cold.

Hope you folks are all well & not working too hard &
not have too cold weather.

Lots & lots of love to everybody,
Tom

Pvt. T. L. Stewart
96th Co., 6th Marines

Letter to Mother, January 15, 1919

Somewhere in France.

Dear Mother:

I am at present at a very small French village and a
very huge army camp called St. Aignon and also the 'mad
house,' mud hole, or anything of that sort would be most
appropriate.

It is a classification camp and re-outfitting center. I am
in class A, have been outfitted & am only waiting for the
word to shove off; I hope back to the outfit, but it is hard
telling where.

This camp is an awful place to stay and I sure hope we
leave soon; have been here a week now. There are about
30,000 men here, all going and coming all the time, so it
has reason to be the mad house they call it.

Above all that, being France, it rains every day, so there
is a fearful mud hole but, if there were no mud, we'd think
we were back in the states I guess.

All the bunch didn't leave Dijon and they all thot I was
a fool for going, and I had to put up quite an argument
at the last to get away. This man's army is sure funny,
isn't it? I sure have some good friends there, both French
and American, I can state that. Ellen wants me to come
back for her wedding this spring, and I certainly shall, if
I can. She and Madame Chapuis have certainly been fine
to me, just as if I were one of the family, and it was not
the easiest always for them, as my French is somewhat

deficient. They insisted when I left that I write them for whatever I need, as America is too far.

One of her sons is with the Americans. I met them both. I also saw the old year out, there, and that is their Xmas, that is when they give presents. Mother Chapuis gave me a splendid billfold and Ellen, a cute silver seal for sealing envelopes with wax, you know, tho what I'll do with it I don't know. It's so darn hard to keep anything in this army that you don't carry right with you all the time.

Was all thru the Hotel de Ville the Sunday before I left, also up in the tower, where you could get a splendid view. It is sure a splendid place; some of the things you can hardly imagine.

I want you some time to write to Madame Chapuis, for she said she was my 'French mother' and she has indeed been a good one to me, and tell her how much I appreciate her. I was simply helpless in French, but she understands. Ellen is splendid too, of course, and her brothers like all Frenchmen quite speedy. Madame A. Chapuis, 2 Quai Nicholas Rollin, (Cote d'Or) Dijon, France. You may write in English, of course, as one of the brothers speaks English and if he is not there, Ellen has several friends who do, provided she does not make it out for herself.

I have lots of time for writing here, but no place for that or anything else. You stand in line here for everything but to draw your breath. So I had to wait for this two foot space at a table and scribble this to you.

I told you I guess that I finally got some letters a few days before I left Dijon. One from you, dad and granny and a couple from Vee. I hope granny is still getting along well and improving still. Is certainly too bad about Will Pine. What is Mrs. Pine doing. Still in the Bank? Or has she gone home to Hepler?

What is Viv doing. I haven't heard from him for a very long time and nobody says anything very definite. I judge he is still at Florence. I met a kid from Denver the other day who knew a couple of kids I do.

I suppose everyone was home for Xmas. I wish I had been in a position to send you all something but circumstance unfortunately prevented.

I expect I'll not know any of my young brothers or sisters when I come back and no doubt they're all already bigger than I am.

I certainly hope I get away from this place soon. I hope to the outfit but any place in preference to this.

Must close this now. I have taken the liberty of writing on both sides of the paper since the censorship is lifted somewhat. I hope the scissors don't ruin it.

Lots and lots of love to everyone.
Tom

Letter to Bob, February 18, 1919

Somewhere in France.

Dear Bob:

Guess you think it about time that I let you know personally that I am still up and coming.

I got the letter you wrote last August, I believe, while you were still at granny's, anyway with your picture in it. Sure looked natural all right. Guess you're still the same little old devil all right. How do you like Spearville? Guess not much any more—too much city life for you.

I'm at Tours, France, now on guard duty again. Have not so much liberty here, tho this is a larger city.

We are a good half hour's walk from town so it's quite a little jog for us.

Have had some pretty cold weather but is back again to the regular chilly rainy days again. Thank goodness it isn't

so muddy here as St. Aignon. I was sure thankful to get
away from there.

Haven't gotten any mail here yet but hope to soon for
goodness knows I must have a lot of it here in France
somewhere.

Had better close this now.

Lots of love to you Bob and the whole family.
Tom

Camp Rochambeau, A.P.O. 717
Censored by J. S. Marrock 2nd lt.

Letter to Folks, February 23, 1919

ON ACTIVE SERVICE WITH THE AMERICAN
EXPEDITIONARY FORCES

Dear Folks,

Nothing doing but the same old drag of 24 on and 24
off, so life is as per usual one darn thing after another.
Have started a little baseball, the first time I've handled
a ball for 2 years or more. Are to have a camp league and
then a star team to represent the camp.

At present tho' its raining a stead April downpour
which precludes most all out door sports except such as
guard duty, practice work etc.

Haven't had any mail yet but am looking for it any day
now as it ought to begin to catch up pretty soon and I sure
must have an armload some where else in France.

I am over in the guard house writing this. No, I'm not
an 'inmate' but on duty. We will have inspection in about
an hour as this is Sunday morning when happen all the
evils that there is no time for on week days.

I have not had much of an opportunity to see much
of Tours. The 'Y' has a theatre here with some good
shows—American product mostly from organizations

over here. They also have a good library and reading room and a restaurant. All this up town. Out at camp hell they have a large entertainment room and a small canteen.

Well, they came near getting the 'Lincoln'of this war too, didn't they; but the "Tigre' is hard to hit.

Well I guess I'd better cut this short for now. Hope everyone is well there.

Lots and lots of love,
Tom

Letter to Helen, April 17, 1919

A.E.F.

Dear Helen:

Tonight I'm a naughty boy and am letting my lessons go 'a la Gare.' I feel like celebrating for I'm now going to all my classes after much insistences. They haven't seemed to insist, at least in some classes and they happened to be the courses that I insisted upon having. Haven't got exactly what I wanted but can't be too particular, I suppose.

My typewriting and accounting at least are practical and I want the French and transportation is interesting to me tho some find it a mighty dry subject. They have good reference books on commerce, finance, etc. here. Up till recently I've only been doing about half enough actual work so have had time to read a little other stuff. Am reading a book on Socialism, also have been reading some of Dr. Manberg on the peace proposition.

Have some pretty strong views on both international and national politics but guess they'd better go un-registered here.

Well really I'd like to know myself why the censorship is still on. The other countries have taken it off. The boys all say so we can't tell the folks at home the straight goods over here.

See somebody at home has gotten out a pamphlet 'treatment of Enlisted Men since the Armistice.' Never mind, things aren't like home but we're none of us suffering any unless perhaps in feelings.

Have been getting mail now fairly regularly the last few days—forwarded from Tours. Doubt if I ever get the back mail; I have written repeatedly for it.

Oh yes, we get rain for a change and also without a change; it makes no dif. A week ago Sunday was a nice day tho.

It is reported that Wilson and Pershing will be here this Sunday—Easter. That means a downpour certainly, for either Easter or inspection would bring it and both!/Ch, la! La!

Here's hoping it's a nice day however, in anticipation of the 3 or 4 hours one 'stands by' on the grounds waiting for them.

Madame, you ask what we eat. I cannot discuss the matter without falling into lingo known as A.E.F. English which is actually spoken not written. However we have a regimental mess, rather than company. We eat 3 times daily however. There are oranges in France, also still some grapes. Dates and figs are abundant; all these are very high as the French are on to the gentle art of 'franc' seducing.

Your little red box of oranges sounds good—both box and oranges.

We have had a touch of March weather lately. Made me think of Kansas all right. Have had several windy days and one night a thunder storm which is very rare in this country—no lightening tho. Have never seen a real electric storm over here yet.

Guess you'll be home before I am all right. Hope I won't be so long behind you tho. Mustn't work too hard not catch the 'flu.' Glad the folks didn't any of them have it badly. Must close.

Lots and lots of love,
Tom

Letter to Dorto, May 1, 1919

Dear Dorto,

J'ai veu votre letter quelque jours passes and was very glad to hear from you again. Have just about a half hour now before the first class this AM so je vous ecris.

Expect you will be a regular Frog by commencement time. Then when I get back if I can't talk American at least I can talk to you. Wish I could be present at your commencement exercises but as it is, guess I will be getting out of this school here only a week before that time. Where to—sais pas—mais souhaite veis Amerique.

The work here is not so very hard, at least I haven't found it so but it is a good thing it isn't, for your military duties conflict so that there is little uninteruptful chance for study.

It has been cold as the deuce here this week. It snowed one day and rained all day yesterday. The hills near here were covered with snow and they are not very high, it was surprising that there would be snow on them this time a year.

To-day is a French holiday—labor day or something. No one is allowed to leave camp. I am hoping to get a week end pass to Dijon and get a good feed ' chey ma marraine' but don't know what sort of luck I'll have. This week we have school on Saturday to show off, to some visitors again.

We had Baker and Pershing last week. I'll stop here for a moment, because a comrade has asked me how to write something for his composition. I give you perfect right to correct my French for, I use a lot of dialect and slang. Thus, I must end here.

Hugs,
Tom

Letter to Mother, May 11, 1919

Beaune, Cote d'Or, France.

Dear Mother,

I have just finished writing a couple of French letters so that I am still thinking a little French, Almost wrote 'fini' for finish, 'ecrire' for write and 'je' for I. I'll try and get it out of my head and relax a little. This is a sweet summer day and spring is sure came. It is perfect almost and I don't think that, simply because we got paid this morning, tho that did make things a bit brighter in some respects.

I was down yesterday to the Hotel God—that is not sacrilege—It is a hospital that was built in the 13th century by a noble of one of the Ducs of Burgundy and has been operated as a hospital ever since. It is needless to say quite different from an American conception of a modern hospital. Wonderful big rooms and not in the least crowded, but only a single row of big poster beds down each side, all with the old fashioned curtains, which really give them each a private ward if they so desire.

There is an order of sisters as nurses. The grounds are nicely laid out with the French jardinieris exact neatness and perfection. The main courtyard sure takes you back to the fourteenth century except that they didn't ask for cigarettes in those days. I only wish I'd had some tho.

There is a small musee up on one of the floors which has some very remarkable old things in it. A many others carried wood slabs that were used in the original structure, ancient furniture, armorers tools, etc, as well as some

statuary and paintings. One picture, really the only one
of note, is quite remarkable in it, everyone here talks so
much about it. By a dutch or Walloon painter subject
matter the judgement day. It is a wonderful wealth of
detail and is very remarkable in that respect. I think I
prefer some of the master's stuff tho. It is not a large
picture but to put a reading glass over it reveals some
marvelous work! The fur and velvet on the robes, for
instance, the textures; the jewels, the faces and in another
picture the printing in a book which is quite small itself in
the picture, are all remarkable. But there is so much detail
that it detracts from it to my idea.

I expect to go to Lyon next week. We go down
with my transportation class. We will be railway
inspectors — getting pretty high up in the world, n'est pas.
Lyon is almost equal to Paris in beauty they say; it is the
second city.

To-day is Mother's Day. Last year mother's day I was
traveling, well I remember, headed for Vitry le Francois
in Champaigne via 40 hommes and 8 cheveaux. To-day
it is better than then. Tho it is nearly as bad. Always an
argument on in the barracks and now it is opposite my
bunk and it is on military training and some of them can
talk pretty loud.

Madame Chapuis said she had had a letter from you
and was going to have me read it to her but we never got
to it. Ellie's future mother-in-law was there and her sons
are coming home now, one is at home now and another is
coming. She probably can't tell you much about any little
town in France. Even tho better educated tend to know
only their own province and Paris. Montfaucon is near
Verdun I think. I have never had a chance to look it up yet.

Last night was over to a doughboy show at the camp
theatre. It was pretty good vaudeville but they are mostly
pretty much the same. I'd like to go to a real theatre once

more. One of the boys said as soon as he gets to N.Y. he's going to hit the first ice cream parlor and buy about $5 worth of ice cream. I think that will hit me about right too.

The Masons are going to have a banquet in about a week, also perhaps a dance. Think I'll attend now that I've gotten paid.

I'm going to try and go down to see a collection of Raemaeker's pictures on the war, on exhibition down in town.

Wilson has said that the whole army will be home by Sept 1st which sure sounds good if only it could be taken for a surety. Hope the Boches sign up and things get settled up so there'll be no more argument.

Guess the Stewart family will soon be assembled, hope I'll be there soon too. Still have no definite information, tho' the 3rd Army men will not go home with this University.

Must close this. The argument is getting too furious I can't think. It's nearly dinner time.

Beau-coup love to everybody and especially to my mother, Tom

E. Co. 11th Prov. Reg.
Am. E.F.U. A.P.O. 909

Letter to Tom's Mother from Madame Chapuis, May 12, 1919

Dijon

Dear Madame,

It is with pleasure that I received your letter, and I undertake to respond to it, one of my friends who knows English well translated the letter for me.

We had the agreeable surprise to see Mr. Tom last Sunday May 4, he had come with permission to Dijon.

He is doing well and he is picking up French customs: he wears a little mustache.

He photographed us with a little apparatus that he received in his Christmas package.

He promised to come see us before June 7 because on that date classes finish at the university.

I received a letter from Miss Vera and I answer her by this same courier.

We are impatient to see the Peace Treaty signed and it is with joy that we celebrate the hour of Allied glory and the fall of Germany.

May peace reign forever on earth and may God send us his blessings.

Receive, dear lady, as well as your family, my best wishes as well as those of my parents.

Your friend in France,
Madame Chapuis

Letter to Helen, May 13, 1919

Beaune, Cote d'Or, France.
Le 13 Mai 1919.

Dear Helen:

Just got your letter tonight, and was tickled green. Mail is beginning to come direct now again. The Tours outfit has broken up so I don't get any forwarded from there any more, tho I know there must be some more there.

Well I take this mail business rather philosophically now having gone without it so much. But when you get mail you keep expecting it and then if you don't you sort of give it up anyway and don't look for any. I hope I get a bunch of it here before the 7 of June when the term closes and I suppose I shove off again!! 'on ne sait pas on.'

I am tempted to put off writing this until tomorrow and write it on the typewriter so you won't be high-toning me; for I'm just getting so I can write a little. I sure hope I can get home before fall again when the 'company' is assembled at Spearville. Must say it doesn't look much as if that would happen so I'll wish for a Thanksgiving or Christmas dinner at home. How is that? I'd rather look at the long end of it and then not be disappointed. I'll state they won't send me on any recruiting duty tho when I get back like they have Stan.

Vee asks just why are they keeping us. Well really they are sending men home much faster than they expected to and are getting them out mighty fast. Just why, the regulars, who also are composed of duration men almost in their entirety, are being held till last, is unknown among the bucks. One should inquire of Pershing, I suppose. Have heard that the 5th, 6th, and 7th are to precede the old timers at that on the sailing list of regulars. That however is only hearsay and not official.

It is quite hot here now and summer weather is on for fair. I am going to Lyon this week end, D.V. and W.P. but in fact in spite of the last for one wouldn't get far if it was allowed.

Last Sunday was out to a little village near here and had supper. A few of the village belles were dancing in the café to mechanical organs. The French make too much work out of dancing tho and entirely too fast. Give me a nice dreamy waltz. I took some pictures out there of some old folks among the chickens and they were sure tickled to death to have their pictures taken.

Also, took a few up at Dijon. Sent them the ones of the family that I had printed so can't send any, but will have to have some more made so you can see my 'belle marraine.' She is 'tres gentile' at least. I wish I could parler decently so they would not think I was such a bore.

My French Prof here makes me see how darn little French I do know. But at least I have a pretty good pronunciation and know a good many common idioms that I wouldn't have learned in books; can make myself understood even if I do murder their grammar.

Every thing is sure pretty over here. If ever you came to France, come between May and September. If you come any other time bring hobnails, caoutchan, umbrella, and hip boots. The lilacs are all in bloom now and there are loads of them and the air is sure filled with their perfume. All kinds of blossoms too and it makes everything so pretty.

Well just now got back. I'll be glad when I get some where they can't enforce attendance to lectures. Even tho they be interesting—and this one was not—one never appreciates what he is forced to hear. Business of leading a horse to water. The fellows are prejudiced already for being forced to attend, so that if it should be good they only make fun and ridicule; oh of course not openly at the theatre for there are officials and many M.P.'s to keep the boys from laughing and clapping at inappropriate intervals. Men are at attention while waiting for the thing to begin.

Will have to stop now for a formation. More formations here than study. I should say that as a university, this is a good Military post. They suppressed an attempt to publish a regimental paper, because a straw vote was taken for president. One hesitates to think what would happen if an attempt were made at a student's council or anything like that. Well only three weeks more.

At the big A.E.F. Shoot over here the Marines took 13 of the 31 gold medals, taking 1st 2nd and 3rd. The 5th Marines took the regimental contest and the second division the divisional contest. A Marine also took first in the pistol shoot. That is rather grabbing things off isn't it?

You are sure some busy kid these days n'est pas? Don't overwork. Make the kids do the work. That's the way it's done in the army. 'Pass the buck" but the buck must do the best he can which usually means keep out of sight. Men are supposed to be babies while in the army, that's all. They are certainly treated that way in every corner.

Well I must close this. It's a way after taps and the lights will be going out pretty soon and I haven't my bunk made up yet.

Lots of love,
Tom

E. Co. 11th Prov. Reg.
Am. E.F.U. A.P.O. 909

I'm sending this to P. C. at Spearville, as I don't know exactly where you will be, not knowing whether it takes 2 or 4 weeks to reach you. They can forward.

T.L.S.

I enclose pictures. Hope they reach you.

Letter to Mother, May 20, 1919

Beaune, France.

Dear Mother:

I scarcely know how to begin this, so I guess I'll start with the least important. Last Friday, I was fortunate enough to get to go to Lyon with a class, thereby getting an extra 24 hours there. Got located and went to a show which did not amount to much, being musical comedy and in French. The comedy would scarcely have gotten across in the states, but these frogs have a peculiar sense of humor.

Saturday A. M. went thru the Bourse—the Board of Trade Bldg. and it is some palace. Can't imagine such

a building in the states for the purpose. But the floor,
or the Pit, I suppose, was diminutive as compared to
Chicago Board of Trade, say those Windy City men who
were with us.

Upon the third floor however is the silk exhibit. Lyon,
before the war, was the world's chief silk, lace, and
embroidery center; they have a wonderful display of
tissues, embroideries, laces, tapestries et cetera.

Some embroideries and tissues in silk that would make
some painting look sick in comparison, so finely and richly
are they done.

There are tapestries and Persian rugs that dealers have
offered as much as a million dollars for. I say dollars for
they are always American; who else is so foolish as to buy
them. They also have a histories room going , from some
of the first fabrics known—Egyptian, about 4000 B.C.
now in a nice state of decay, but still intact; all up thru
most every century to the present time. There is a piece
of the coronation gown of the wife of Napoleon I in heavy
silk, heavily embroidered and richly brocaded in gold.
Models of weaving machines from the earliest date up to
the modern ones now in use.

Then in the PM, I went out to the Roman aqueducts,
about an hour's ride from town with a "Y" party. There
are about 90 arches standing; more than usually seen
together. I took a few pictures but the light was bad. Don't
know how they will come out.

There is certainly some masonry in them to be still
standing. They are made up of small blocks of hard stone.
I rather had the impression that large building stone was
used. The duct itself was still intact in some places tho the
covering was all gone.

Saturday night then I went to the Theatre, Guiamell
Tell. I'd better stop there for I can never do justice to any
kind of description. In French, of course, so I had to try to

remember the story, but the singing was wonderful and easily the best I've ever heard. The theatre is more modern and seems more like the U.S.A. It is extremely beautiful nevertheless, tho scarcely any larger than the one at Dijon. Orchestra was wonderful, like a great pipe organ.

Sunday AM went up the hill to the cathedral. It is modern—built in 1877-84 and not entirely finished yet. It is a combination of architecture so the guide book says. The interior is rich in decorations and very elaborate, Byzantium, I guess. It is different from so many of the old, old ones.

The chapel downstairs is as large as most churches in the city. We went down the hill then thru a pretty park. The hill is quite steep, a bluff in fact. Went up on cog road. Then went out to the park which was very pretty, but I was a little disappointed in it. It is so noted—supposed to be one of the finest in Europe. Guess a fellow looks for too much when they put it up that way.

After that I took an early train and got home about nine o'clock tho could have made one at five AM

Now then the important part begins. I arrive at the barracks and one friend of mine erstwhile a third loot' recently commissioned had been to Paris and brought—my Mail!

Well there were four bundles and considerably over a hundred letters in all. Some over a year old and some as late as Feb. It had been at Headquarters of Marines in Paris where I have written time and again for it.

Well, I haven't done any studying since; I've been reading mail and this PM, Tuesday, just finished reading, and now find myself in a helpless position trying to answer a year's mail in a day in a letter. It made me so darn Homesick, I can hardly see thru. You folks all have been so good to me and here I am half the time not writing and then only a scribbly note.

Sure learned a thousand and one things almost and
does seem sort of funny reading some mail written May
5th etc. of last year. Dad has sure written me some of the
dandiest letters. Do wish I had been getting them all right
along. Got the pictures Po and Uncle Freddy sent last year
at this time, also one of dad and some kodak ones that Do
and Lucy sent. Also one adorable one of Mary Myers. Poor
Mary! All the letters telling about Will Pine's death and
Paul's too and all the news at home for a year. It's pretty
nearly enough to make a guy homesick, isn't it?

I've stuck up for France long enough and you can bet
I wouldn't trade a foot of the U.S.A. for all of it. Tho I
still insist it could be appreciated if you weren't in the
army. It's pretty but oh Lord but it's rotten over here.
What a relief to get home you can't know. Know how
good it would seem to step out on a clean sidewalk of a
broad street in a sunshiny city and not forever meeting
Mademoiselles with the eternal 'combien eyes' and not
have to turn your head every time you pass a frog to keep
from being gassed with garlic fumes.

Don't tell me what is the national flower of France. I
want to go where they don't eat snails and horse meat,
nor call a doctor when they see you down a glass of water;
and have a few silver dollars in my pocket instead of this
United Cigar Store coupons stuff. But most of all I want a
blue serge suit in place of this one I've got.

Mama, dear, I'm sorry for that foolish letter about
publishing my letters. I was sorry after I sent it. But I
didn't like seeing all the stuff I wrote in print.

If I had had any notion last winter of being here this
long, I'd have had the bank and dad send me statements
that I was needed at home, but no use now I guess, for
even the division leaves in July they say; and that will be
the latest possible date unless that should be changed. I
have remote chance of coming home with the University

but it is so indefinite that I can hardly count on it. Will mean about a month sooner. But again, being a Marine, you see, makes it highly improbable for they are hardly ever moved with the army like that. That was why I couldn't come home from St. Aignon last winter. I really had some hopes of it tho I never said so for it was so doubtful.

It has been reported here that some papers in the states have published statements that this camp — the University — was a camouflaged camp.

The regulars are now supposed to go home with Pershing in the spring or July rather. At any rate you take it from me, the men in the divisions are by far better off than those not, in the majority of cases.

The other day at the Le Mans shoot, the 2nd took the divisional contest. The 5th Marines the Regimental, a Marine co., the machine gun contest. A Marine first in the pistol contest. Marines took first, second, and third in the individual honors and 13 out of 21 gold medals. Shouldn't be quite so grabby you say? Well they can't be beaten. The 2nd suffered more casualties than any other division. Took more prisoners than the closest three divisions — 1/4 of the total — more cannon and more ground. Was second only to one division in machine guns captured — the 3rd. Have received more foreign decorations than any division. And three times as many American decorations than any other. Fought on more fronts than any other, its closest competitor the 1st missed Champaigne. So it is a division to be proud of after all. But this is simply statistics published in the Stars and Stripes and need not be repeated. It gets so tiresome over here hearing every one tell how his division won the war singlehanded. And all arguments only cause hard feeling, so as far as possible we try to maintain silence.

The army, of course not all of them, say of that little scrap at Chateau Thierry 'twas all the Marines ever did. But they were on every front and in every fight after that too and lost more men in their own brigade than some of the crack divisions did.

Stanley must have sprung a fine line on you all after reading your letters. You'd think he and I stopped the whole German army at Chateau Thierry to read your letters.

Never mind that old stuff. All I want is to get home; and it's not a hero you're getting—for after all I was in only the one little scrap—but still the same Tom—a bit more sophisticated perhaps and I hope a bit bigger and broader in a good many ways. But it's a cinch no one will be able to say of him again 'nice boy.' I sadly fear that's been 'nest' in this man's army.

I never looked Zeno up because buck privates do not usually go visiting lieutenants.

Don't think I was passing anything up by still writing private before my name. I'm satisfied. Big Bank Presidents and railroad Pres. have it on their door.I did not consider it worth while writing back for the uncertain position of a 'war corporal' tho doubtless there is a paper for me some where.

As for decorations—how do you get that way? The division has been decorated a number of times. I don't know what authority there is for some that are seen over here tho.

I'm hoping to get home before I put on another chevron on my left sleeve in July. There was a frog about half shot that crowded into our car up from Lyon. He showed us his papers—every frog has beaucoup decorations—they live on them with a little 'pan & vin'—but said he never wore them and added 'Les chiens se portent maintenant' 'the dogs are wearing them' now. About like German Iron Crosses.

There seems to be about a million things that I wanted to say but they go wandering when I start to write. Don't kid me about Irven Cobb. Makes me think how Madame Chapiers said I wrote my letter to her in faultless French and then when I look over the handed back composition in class, I know what a 'menteuse' she must have been but forgive her kindly.

I feel no end of a criminal tho for I've gotten some letters and such nice ones too from folks that I've neglected terribly and I can imagine what they must think of me.

Just was over to supper. They threw beans and cold tomatoes at us and that has deprived me entirely of any inspiration I may have had to write. Also hear that those of the 1st 2nd and 3rd division would not be returned with the University. But these tales reverse themselves nearly every day so I'm standing fast and believing nothing.

I believe now I'll stop tho and go down town to see if they have my pictures done so I can enclose some.

Well back again, was up town and back and took a bath. Got a lesson. Is quite an accomplishment, that getting a lesson. For nobody much cares any more—profs or students—if there are any lessons, for they are too close to going home. The profs say it's here for you and you can take it or leave it. I missed the citizenship lecture tonight. It is a terrible bore. Some old fogies have the military authority to compel attendance to some of their rantings.

I also had a recent letter from Vera, also one from Lois. They were dated about April 30th so I'm pretty well posted on modern history now as well.

Well since this has become a volume already I think I had better close. I know there are a lot of other things I meant to say but they've escaped me for the present. I'll write again soon and try to pick up the details. Will write to granny and Emmie soon too. Loads and loads of love to every body and especially you and dad,

Tom

E. Co. 11th Prov. Reg.
A.E.F.U. A.P.O. 909

CHAPTER EIGHT
OCCUPATION FORCE

AFTER THE SIGNING of the armistice on November 11, Germany was given 31 days to evacuate Belgium, France, Luxemburg, and Alsace-Lorraine. They were also forced to withdraw their armies from the Rhineland, and a neutral zone 40 kilometers from the river.[85] The area was then controlled by Allied armies of occupation that garrisoned at three principal crossings of the Rhine: Mainz, Koblenz, and Cologne.[86]

The American 3rd Army moved towards Germany on November 17, 1918, entering the country on November 20. A few days later, the 4th Division entered Koblenz as the first American troops in the Occupation Zone. On December 13, the Americans crossed the Rhine on a pontoon bridge to occupy the eastern edge of the river.[87] The 96th Company then marched up to Rheinbrohl where they were billeted as they awaited their time to return home.

Meanwhile, Tom was being reassigned once more after the closing of the American University at Beaune. Back on April 23, 1919 orders had been received detailing that Tom could attend the University until his courses were completed, then he would be transferred back to the 4th Marine Brigade. So, upon the closing of the University, Tom and two other Marines that had been attending courses at Beaune went to get their orders to return

---

85 Alfred E. Cornebise, "Der Rhein Entlang: The American Occupation Forces in Germany, 1918-1923, A Photo Essay," *Military Affairs* 46, no. 4 (December, 1982): 183.

86 Harry R Rudin, *Armistice 1918* (New Haven: Yale University Press, 1944), 426.

87 Alfred Cornebise, 184.

to their units. However, when the men visited the sergeant to receive them, as Tom said in his interview "he seemed a bit leery and wouldn't hand them over."

Not being deterred, as soon as the sergeant was distracted with a phone call, Tom and the men snatched the travel orders off the table and left. At this time, travel orders for a soldier were his permit to ride the train in 3rd class. So instead of going back to their outfit, Tom and the men got on a train to Marseilles. In Marseilles, they enjoyed a day in the busy port city where "it was said you could see a citizen of any city in the world on the streets."[88] They took a boat ride around Devils Island in the harbor. Then, on their way back north, they decided that they wanted to see the Alps. So, they went over to Chamonix at the base of Mont Blanc and "just stepped across the border line into Switzerland."[89] They then traveled to Paris. While in the city, Tom visited the Louvre, Versailles, and went to the opera to see *Faust*. Tom also mentions that Notre Dame cathedral was still covered in sand bags at the time of their visit.[90]

Finally, the men took a train to the 2nd Division headquarters in Koblenz. From there, Tom rejoined his unit at Rheinbrohl on June 19, 1919. The Marines were billeted in the train station and could visit the town or other villages along the Rhine. However, the Marines were not allowed to have any communication with the German villagers. According to Tom, the only thing to do was to buy beer because the shelves were bare in the shops with the food being scarce and rationed to the Germans. On June 27 to 29, the Marines marched 30 kilometers into the neutral zone to put pressure on the German government to sign the peace treaty, then marched back to the Rhine. While stationed at Rheinbrohl, the big source of entertainment was the Fourth of July celebration. Bands from all units played in the neighbor-

---

88 Tom's Memoir

89 Ibid.

90 Ibid.

hoods all day and at night the 17th Field Artillery fired flares and rockets into the air for a grand pyrotechnics show.[91] The Marines remained in the Occupation Force until July 16.

Letter to Vee, June 16, 1919

AMERICAN RED CROSS

Dear Vee:

I have some very interesting things to tell you both pleasant and otherwise but since I do not know if this will be read or not, I will resist as it is necessary I suppose. You think I'm teasing you writing this way but only want to let you know I'm all right but haven't much chance to write this past week.

What do you think of the Peace situation now. Interesting anyway. Pas vrai?

I may be writing you next time from an adjutants hotel, compris? Ask a soldier.

At present I am at Nevers where I took a chance from Beaune to look up Lt. Branch's grave (Mary M's husband) and took a picture of it. Hated to be here at Beaune so long and not make the attempt.

Will not be able to try to look up Paul's on the way up to Germany as this attempt to-day was un-successful. That is the sorriful news. The other doesn't matter and can wait.

I will doubtless get a courts-martial for absent without leave, but don't worry that sounds big to someone outside the army but on the inside most everyone got 'em so why care.

Had better close this now.

Lots and lots of love,
Tom

---

91 "First American Fourth of July on Banks of Rhine is Marked by Joyful Celebrations of Troops," *The Amaroc News*, July 5, 1919.

Letter to Mother, June 20, 1919

Dear Mother:

Well I got up here in time to make a nice hike
for everything is on the move to shove on over into
Allemagne. We are now in a town named Herschback at
the edge of the neutral zone.

Had a pretty hot day for a hike but it rained the
night before so was not so awful dusty in the morning.
Considering I had been on the train for several days and
hadn't been feeding regularly I got along fine and don't
feel nearly so stiff today as I expected to. Now all my
French is useless again. I start to speil French at them
every time I have a thing to say.

We stayed all night at Metz which is a very pretty old
town; wide streets and clean and modern. That is as the
little we saw appeared.

We came Dijon to Nancy to Metz to Luxemburg, Trives
and Coblentz then Neuweit and after that had to catch our
outfits as they had started to move.

I can't see so much difference in the towns here and
in France. Maybe a shade cleaner but don't get the
goldhandled mess kit for cleanliness at that. Saw a few
good looking Frauleins on the way up but none here.

Can't buy anything here (except shoe polish which
seems to be quite necessary). Makes no difference tho
for I'm broke. Guess you folks think that is my regular
state of finances. Seems I'm always saying so, but don't
need any. Spent all my money seeing the country while
at Beaune. Not many of the old fellows I knew here any
more and have seen a few officers I knew in the battalion
or regiment, but none in the company.

The country is very wooded and the soil looks more like
out home than in France. Along the Rhine tho it is pretty

rocky and they raise grapes as in France. It's sure possible to fall off your farm too the way they terrace them up.

We haven't much of a place here. Thirteen men where the deutch say 6 have been using, but then some of the rest of the battalion are out in the open so we are lucky I guess. Anyway soon after Monday, we will either go on or, if peace is signed we hope — back to where the outfit were before, which they say is a fine place.

I sent a bunch of cards. I hope you get them all. I'll send a few more of Metz. Wish I could send some of everything I've seen. Have taken quite a few pictures too but there is no chance to have them developed, so may have to wait till I get to the states.

Was pretty lucky the other day in Paris. Saw, I guess about every one I knew there, not many of course — simply happened to run on to them.

Went thru the Louvre this time. The Invalides and the Clumy Museum, also up to the top of Eiffel Tower. My pal in school there also took us all over the Latin Quarter.

Last but not least, we went to "Faust" at the Opera. The piece itself, I did not appreciate quite as much as some, but we did not have the best of seats, not having beaucoup francs and prices running a bit like N. Y. But the building and the Foyer are worth the price of admission, especially the latter.

When I get to the states, I'll write a lot more perhaps or better save it and tell you.

Not much else to write I guess but my address is 96th Co., 6th Reg., U. S. Marines, A.E.F. At least I hope to be sailing before mail has a chance for a round trip — that has been six weeks with me so far every time. May get some forwarded from the University but haven't much confidence any more in getting mail forwarded.

I mean to write you at once again as soon as the "Y" comes up or we go back, for haven't a good place at all so far. Must close.

Lots and lots of love,
Tom

Letter to Vera, July 7, 1919

Dear Vera:

I'm sending another package. There's nothing in this one except a bit of stuff I rather want to keep and it is superfluous to carry around since they are making so many inspections and you have to carry all your earthly goods when you roll your pack, for the officers come thru and salvage everything left in the billet while we are out to drill.

Of course if you're shy anything tho—well that's your hard luck—no issue but you'd better get it or you won't go home.

Well I'm O.K. now if I can only hold on to all I've got.

There is just a bunch of letters and other junk. My watch also. Can take it out and have it cleaned. That is all it needs and some one can wear it till I get back. There is no place here I can have it fixed.

No news as always, so had better ring off for now.

Lots of love,
Tom

Letter to Margaret, July 11, 1919

Dear Margaret:

Got your dandy letter of the first of June a day or two ago. It was one of the very few that have been forwarded from Beaune. I am not complaining tho for expect to be home soon, when mail matters will be revolutionized for us and I hope it won't be long after I'm back till I see you, but one never can tell in this Marine Corp.

Well Bob you should have seen us the other day getting de-cootie-ized. They have a big steam boiler that looks like a steam engine, without the engine, and we put our clothes in a big steel basket and shove them in and wait a half an hour while the steam is on.

In the meantime ye Marines stand around Paris Island style; that is with a towel, or trousers, in fact most anything, which is not much. And the folks on the excursion boats going by must look the other way. Fortunately they are nearly all soldiers tho, so 'Se ne fait rien' or 'es macht nichte uas' as Jerry puts it.[92]

Today we could see, on the other side of the river, a column of horses as far as you could see in both directions—the Second is turning in their livestock.

I met a couple of fellows here out of my old boot company on Paris Island the other day. One had just come back from river patrol.

We are having a life of inspection now and it will continue till we shove. Have to have everything on the 'list' down to shoe strings and it's impossible to get an issue of anything. Oh yes they come and take your name and that's the last of it. But you'd better get it or you'll get a good bawling out. Nobody steals anything in the army tho. They just 'salvage' it.

You'd have laughed the other day if you'd seen what was on a bulletin board on my post when I was on guard. Some one had cut out a full page ad from a Detroit paper of the U. S. Army recruiting office telling all the joys and advantages of serving on the Rhine now. Oh boy—it's sure fine over here—it said so in the ad and I'm sure they wouldn't deceive any one.

---

92 "It does not matter."

Well it hadn't been up an hour till some one had a neat black crepe rosette and streamers on it. So every body stopped and looked and listened then.

Well it's nearly taps and Tommy's blanket is not laid out on the soft pine yet. But these darn Heinies (or the French either) won't use soft pine. They all have hard wood floors. Would be the envy of any one in the states, but they are poor bunks.

Lots and lots of love, Bob.
Tom

Letter to Vee, July 12, 1919

AMERICAN EXPEDITIONARY FORCES
YOUNG MEN'S CHRISTIAN ASSOCIATION
ARMY OF OCCUPATION

Dear Vee:

Don't be surprised at anything I send home in a letter; for the situation is that I have to send anything I want to keep, that is at all unhandy to carry.

Can send no more packages from here now.

Just heard a good one. Friend girl in U.S.A. writes Buck thusly: "How is it that you're only a private?" He writes back "How is it you only work in a 5 and 10 cent store?"

Must close this. Am sending a Second Division hand book. Hope it reaches you. It has the facts about the 2nd from its organization till July 1st this year.

Love,
Tom

CHAPTER NINE
THE RETURN HOME

ON JULY 17, 1919 the 96th Company entrained to begin their journey home. According to Tom, their first stop was Cologne where they remained on the train. Then the Marines traveled through Belgium and northern France, where they "did not see a town or village that was not completely or partially destroyed."[93] They finally arrived at Brest, France on the 21st. The Marines then waited at Camp Pontanezen outside of town for their transport home. During their wait, the Knights of Columbus provided entertainment for the soldiers through carnivals. The program put on included: the K.C. Girls, an organization of lady musicians, Mr. E. Jerome, monologist, George Lemothe, a champion swordsman, Mr. R. Thompson, in a unique ragalogue, and the Jersey City police quartet.[94]

Letter to Dad, July 22, 1919

THE SALVATION ARMY
WITH THE AMERICAN TROOPS IN FRANCE

Dear Dad,

I got your letter of July 6 yesterday which is about the best time any has gotten to me yet. We are at Camp Pontanezen, Brest, supposed to be the largest camp in Europe. Brest is living up to its rep in true form and it is raining today. We did see the sun at times, yesterday, however. We are going through inspection all over again

---

93 Interview with David Kirk.

94 "'Bon Voyage' Troupe Entertains Yanks on Ships in the Harbor," *The Pontanezen Duckboard*, July 23, 1919.

here, of course. But I only wish our officers would take a tip from them. It is the first time we ever got off without waiting 2 or 3 hours for the inspecting officer. They inspected our packs and full equipment this A. M. in about ten minutes (per company). We used to have to put in at least two hours for the same thing and a terrible lot of fuss for fear you wouldn't have your canteen placed at exactly the right spot, etc.

Had our coal oil bath & physical inspection yesterday.

There is plenty of amusement here. A half dozen big ships with entertainment most every afternoon and evening in each. A big Salvation Army hut where I am writing this. The K.C. has a free carnival every evening out in one of the open lots and it is always crowded.

The chow is the same old canned bill etc. that you expect at a place like this and have to put up with & you go thru by the numbers like at St. Aignon; only you haven't got to wait around hours in the mud as we did last winter.

You spoke of Aunt Maude going to be at Spearville. I guess I'll hardly make it in July and if she is gone, I might meet her some place on the way home, Chi or K.C. I figure on stopping off at Aunt Minnie's.

Well, I had to see Paris and I'll venture half the men over here were never there and at least 2/3 of the men who were out of the divisions, who saw it, either were there a.w.o.l. or in a hospital. Oh, you never get anything in this outfit unless you take it, that's contrary to the well-known army slogan.

I heard one of the fellows say they were paying a dollar an hour for harvest hands so wasn't surprised at the jack Viv is raking down. But at a guaranteed price for wheat I guess the farmers should worry.

Bet Bob gets her fill of sauerkraut and sow belly. Tell her I'll talk my dutch to her & my french to Do. Sure some lingo an American has. How he's going to get rid of it is the big question. Just got handed a couple of nice new clean shin plasters. Think I'll send them; if I carry them they'll get mussed. Glad I didn't even collect any souvenirs. They sure make life a nightmare for a chap trying to get them by. He has to stay up nights thinking of new ways to camouflage them.

Well, must close this now.

Lots of love,
Tom

T. L. Stewart
96th Co., 6th Marines
APO 710

The Marines waited until the 25th when they were able to board the USS *George Washington*. However, the ship was too large to dock in the port so the Marines were taken out to it and climbed ladders to get aboard. As the ship was leaving the harbor, Major General Helmick, Base Commander of Brest, Brigadier General Smedley D. Butler, several other officers, a French General, and three boats with bands bid farewell and escorted the Marines out of the harbor.[95] Aboard the ship was a plethora of passengers all anxiously awaiting the return home.

These included the Second Division units: Second Division Headquarters, Third Infantry Brigade Headquarters, Fourth Marine Brigade Headquarters, Fifth Regiment Marines, Second Battalion Sixth Marines, and the 322nd Field Signal Battalion. Next, General officer passengers: Major General John A. Lejeune commanding the 2nd Division, Major General R. Noble, Medical Corps, and Brigadier General Wendell C. Neville commanding the Fourth Marine Brigade. Then, Non-Second Division passengers: the Brest Casual Company 3209, 130 members of the

---

95 "French Escort Ship From Brest Harbor," *The Hatchet*, July, 26, 1919.

Army Nurse Corps, the Hoover civilian employees, and around six hundred officers and men with brides. Finally, livestock passengers, which included several Marine mascots: three fawns, one fox, one monkey, one anteater, one burro, two kittens, and about thirty dogs.[96]

The sailing was much smoother than when the 96th arrived in France, since the ship did not have to follow a zig-zag pattern to avoid subMarines. During the trip, the Marines were entertained by several means. They could attend a movie on board, go to the theater and see skits acted out by other Marine units, or they could attend boxing matches held on the deck of the ship. They sailed until August 3, when the ship docked in New York City.

Postcard to Folks, August 3, 1919

Docked 6 PM 9 days enroute. Good passage. Two days quite rough. Will write. No discharge before 10th I think. Going to Camp Mills.

Once the Marines landed, they marched out to Camp Mills, Long Island. They were in camp for five days. During this time, Tom visited, and subsequently disappointed by, Coney Island. On August 8, the men paraded as part of the 2nd Division up 5th Avenue in New York City. After finishing the parade, they took a train back to Quantico, Virginia. On the 12th, they paraded through Washington DC and were reviewed by President Woodrow Wilson. The next day, August 13, 1919, Tom was given a new uniform, given an allotment of five cents a mile to get back to his point of enlistment, given a $60 bonus for being honorably discharged, and then sent on his way home.[97]

---

96 "Mascots, Matrons, Maids, Military in Floating City," *The Hatchet*, July 26, 1919.

97 William Brown Meloney, *Where Do We Go From Here*, New York: Thomsen-Ellis Press, 1919.

Tom made his way up through D.C one last time and headed West. Along the way, he stopped off one day to visit his aunt, Minnie Stewart. After returning to Spearville, he returned to his job at the First National Bank. Unbeknownst to him, the bank deposited ten percent of his salary into his account every month he was in service. He remained employed at the bank for a year until he received a letter from Stanley William's brother-in-law, Claude McConnell. The letter was a job offer at McConnell's new wholesale candy and tobacco company in Okmulgee, Oklahoma with Stanley. He was offered much higher pay, association with Stanley again, and he did not want to work the wheat harvest any longer, so he took the job.

Tom moved to Okmulgee and worked as a bookkeeper for the company. His diligent work saved the company during the depression and they continued to operate successfully. During this time, Tom met Dorothy Allison and they were married on June 10, 1927. They had two children, Thomas Leidigh Stewart Jr. (1930) and Carolyn Stewart Kirk (1931). Tom and Dorothy moved to Oklahoma City in 1977.

Tom passed away in Oklahoma City on April 9, 1993 at the age of 98. Throughout his life, he believed in being physically fit, stemming from his early Marine training, he always gave respect, paid attention to the way he talked to others, understood sacrifice, and always had good humor. He led a quiet, productive life, kept God's commandments and nurtured his children to do the same. Tom is buried in Memorial Park Cemetery in Oklahoma City, Oklahoma.

ABOUT THE AUTHOR

JAMES P GREGORY JR. was born in Ada, Oklahoma in 1995 and moved around the state until graduating from Piedmont High School in 2013. In May of 2017 he graduated from the University of Central Oklahoma with a Bachelor's degree in History: Museum Studies and a Bachelor's in Humanities. He is currently a graduate student once more at the University of Central Oklahoma in the Museum Studies program.

BIBLIOGRAPHY

Amaroc News. "First American Fourth of July on Banks of Rhine is Marked by Joyful Celebrations of Troops." July 5, 1919.

Boghardt, Thomas. "Chasing Ghosts in Mexico: The Columbus Raid of 1916 and the Politicization of U.S. Intellgence During World War I." *Army History.* U.S. Army Center of Military History, Fall 2013.

Cale, Harrison. "The American Marines at Verdun, Chateau Thierry, Bouresches, and Belleau Wood." *Indiana Magazine of History 15,* no. 2 (June, 1919): 179-191.

Cornebise, Alfred E. Cornebise. "Der Rhein Entlang: The American Occupation Forces in Germany, 1918-1923, A Photo Essay." *Military Affairs* 46, no. 4 (December, 1982): 183-189.

Dunton, Orley. "Mussing Up The Prussian Guard." *Hearst's Magazine,* December, 1918.

Farwell, Byron. *Over There: The United States in the Great War.* New York: W.W. Norton and Company, 1999.

Freidel, Frank. *Over There: The Story of America's First Great Overseas Crusade.* New York: McGraw-Hill, 1990.

Hatchet. "French Escort Ship From Brest Harbor," July, 26, 1919.

Meloney, William Brown. *Where Do We Go From Here.* New York: Thomsen-Ellis Press, 1919.

Nelson, James Carl. *I Will Hold: The USMC Legend Clifton B. Cates, from Belleau Wood to Victory in the Great War.* New York: New American Library, 2016.

Pontanezen Duckboard. "'Bon Voyage' Troupe Entertains Yanks on Ships in the Harbor." July 23, 1919.

Rudin, Harry R. *Armistice 1918.* New Haven: Yale University Press, 1944.

Seldon, Kevin. "The Battle of Belleau Wood: America's Indoctrination into 20th Century Warfare." Master's thesis, University of Central Oklahoma, 2010.

Stewart, Thomas. "The Story of One Marine." Memoir.

Thomas Stewart, interviewed by David Kirk, 1980s, Transcript.

United States Marine Corps. *History of the 96th Company, 6th Marine Regiment in World War I*. Washington DC: U.S. Marine Corps.1967.

U.S. Marine Corps Muster Rolls: 1893-1958. Microfilm Publication T977, 460 rolls, Records of the U.S. Marine Corps, Record Group 127, National Archives in Washington D.C.

U.S. War Department. *The War With Germany: A Statistical Summary*. Washington D.C.: U.S. GPO, 1919.

Voorhees, Oscar M. "The American Expeditionary Forces University at Beaune: An American University in France." *The Phi Beta Kappa Key* 3, no. 12 (May, 1919): 580-83.

Yockelson, Mitchell. "They Answered the Call: Military Service in the United States Army During World War I, 1917-1919." *Prologue* 30, no. 3 (Fall 1998). www.archives.org

INDEX

To see more of Tom's photos,
visit the Facebook page
"The Story of One Marine"

www.hellgatepress.com

.

CPSIA information can be obtained
at www.ICGtesting.com
Printed in the USA
LVHW01s0804280518
578667LV00009B/644/P